LEARNING TO READ

LEARNING TO READ

A Cognitive Approach to Reading
and Poor Reading

JOHN R. BEECH

Department of Psychology,
University of Leicester

CROOM HELM
London & Sydney

COLLEGE-HILL PRESS, INC
San Diego, CA 92105

© 1985 John R. Beech
Croom Helm Ltd, Provident House, Burrell Row,
Beckenham, Kent BR3 1AT
Croom Helm Australia Pty Ltd, First Floor,
139 King Street, Sydney, NSW 2001, Australia

British Library Cataloguing in Publication Data

Beech, John R.
   Learning to read : a cognitive approach to
   reading and poor reading.
   1. Reading disability 2. Reading –
   Remedial teaching
   I. Title
   371.91'4   B1050.5
   ISBN 0-7099-3291-X

College-Hill Press, Inc,
4284 41st Street
San Diego, CA 92105

Library of Congress Cataloging in Publication Data

Beech, John R.
   Learning to Read

   Bibliography: p.
   Includes index
   1. Reading disability 2. Reading - remedial teaching
3. Title
LB1050.5.B43   1985   372.4'3
84-21421
ISBN 0-88744-110-6

Printed and bound in Great Britain by
Biddles Ltd, Guildford and King's Lynn

CONTENTS

PREFACE

Much has unfolded in terms of our knowledge about the reading process. The research effort in reading has been substantial over the last 60 years, but in recent years the pace has accelerated. Psychologists from other research backgrounds have become interested in the problems of reading and the result has been to enrich the field and to provide new perspectives.

The aim of this book is to discuss research up to the present time on the problems facing children learning to read. It focusses in particular on those children who despite normal intelligence still experience considerable difficulty with acquiring the necessary reading skills. As will be seen, there are several directions that have been taken. As we explore each avenue I hope to draw conclusions which will directly help those in the classroom.

I would like to thank Dr. Jane Oakhill of the MRC Perceptual and Cognitive Unit, University of Sussex, who kindly commented on a draft chapter and my mother, Fran, who is a primary school teacher, for reading the full draft and making comments.

This book was written at the New University of Ulster while I was a lecturer there. I would like to thank my colleagues at Coleraine for the intellectual stimulation they have provided over the years and wish them all the best in the future.

ACKNOWLEDGEMENTS

Permissions by the following sources for
reproduction of illustrations is gratefully
acknowledged.

Academic Press, Inc.
Figure 5.2: Benson, D. F. (1981). Alexia and the
neuroanatomical basis of reading. In F. J.
Pirozzolo and M. C. Wittrock (eds.),
Neuropsychological and cognitive processes in
reading, Copyright (c) 1981 by Academic Press.

NFER-Nelson, Ltd.
Table Al: Shearer, S. and Apps, R. (1975). A
restandardization of the Burt-Vernon and Schonell
Graded Word Reading Tests. Educational Research,
18, 67 - 73. Copyright (c) 1975 by NFER-Nelson.

Oxford University Press, Inc.
Figure 5.3: DeArmond, S. J., Fusco, M. M. and Dewey,
M. M. (1976). Structure of the human brain: a
photographic atlas. Copyright (c) 1976 by Oxford
University Press.

Pergamon Press, Ltd.
Figure 5.6: Galaburda, A. M. (1982). Neuroanatomical
aspects of language and dyslexia. In Y. Zotterman
(ed.), Dyslexia: neuronal, cognitive and
linguistic aspects. Copyright (c) 1982 by
Pergamon Press.

Routledge and Kegan Paul, Ltd
Figure 5.5: Marin, O. S. M. (1980). Appendix 1. CAT
scans of five deep dyslexic patients. In M.
Coltheart, K. Patterson, and J. C. Marshall
(eds.), Deep dyslexia. Copyright (c) 1980 by

Routledge and Kegan Paul.

Chapter One

AN INTRODUCTION

For most of us reading is an effortless process which enables us to gather information at a rapid rate, faster, in fact, than if we were listening to someone saying the same message. However, a significant proportion of the adult population cannot read with such ease. In many cases this is not due to deficiencies in intelligence, nor is it entirely due to poor schooling. Why, in this age of schooling until at least the age of 16, should there be a segment of the population which has experienced such difficulty in learning to read?

To the researcher in reading problems it is of particular interest that there is a proportion of children who are poor readers and who are no less intelligent than children of the same age who are normal readers. Consequently, researchers have been careful to account for the role of intelligence within their working definition of the reading disabled child. One idea is that a child is considered to be behind in reading if his reading is considerably behind what would be expected on the basis of his level of intelligence. This concept is central to our examination of the poor reader, as in most of the studies reviewed here, the effects of intelligence are controlled by making comparison with a control group matched in intelligence with the poor readers.

This book is aimed at reviewing research on the poor reader. A child classified as "dyslexic" comes under the classification of being a poor reader, but is usually defined more specifically than this. Because of the confusion usually surrounding this particular issue, the next chapter is devoted to a more detailed discussion of this topic. All that might be noted here is that both poor readers (as

1

defined here) and dyslexics are poor at reading and are not unintelligent. The dyslexic is further defined to embrace a much smaller sample of children in which other possible factors such as poor home background are eliminated.

After discussing the dyslexia issue and also the prevalence of reading problems, we will examine how reading is normally taught in our schools. Generally speaking, teachers are fairly eclectic in their approach to reading instruction. Usually they use one or two reading schemes but embellish these with their own materials. Hopefully, they try to identify problem areas for some children and give further guidance in these areas. When a teacher is dealing with the same children day after day, a great deal of ingenuity is required to maintain an adequate interest level for the children. In the early stages this is achieved by allowing a great deal of freedom to play towards the end of the school day. For the normal child who progresses easily with reading, the information extracted from the reading materials becomes of interest in its own right. In the case of the poor reader, the incentive is not the same, especially when he becomes segregated from the rest of the class in order to be given extra reading tuition. Consequently it becomes even more important to sustain interest via rewards and incentives which have particular relevance to each poor reader.

If our knowledge about reading were more advanced, we would by now be using screening tests in order to predict which children are probably going to experience difficulties in the future. It is likely that early intervention would amply repay these early remedial efforts. Unfortunately, we do not have this precision at the moment, but the day is approaching when this will become a reality.

The core of the book is concerned with the factors underlying reading disability. Particular emphasis is given to such cognitive factors as verbal and visual processing. As a broad generalization, it seems that poor readers are deficient particularly at lower levels of verbal processing. They are less advanced in their ability to articulate words, to identify the individual sounds in words and in remembering sequences of words, such as in trying to remember a telephone number. They also demonstrate some deficiences in visual processing, but it is difficult sorting out whether this is due to any real visual processing

difficulty or to their translating visual
information into a verbal message. So their visual
difficulties might also be due to poor verbal
processing.

One view of the problem of poor reading is that
the poor reader is lagging behind in the development
of certain cognitive processes crucial to learning
to read. Some might regard this view as somewhat
fatalistic as it might imply that one has only to
wait until the child is a little older before the
teaching of reading can begin. However, teaching
certain underlying cognitive skills may be a way of
accelerating progress. From the viewpoint of the
child, it is much better to try to keep up with
one's contemporaries rather than joining a younger
class. Another viewpoint that might also be
regarded as fatalistic is one suggesting that
certain areas of the brain of the poor reader are
damaged in some manner. As will be seen, post
mortems on two retarded readers have indicated
abnormalities in both cases; however, this is too
small a sample to be conclusive. Even if there is
evidence for brain damage, the plasticity of the
brain is such that given adequate training, one
would hope that a child with reading problems could
still learn to read.

There is much clearer evidence that in the
adult, at least, specific parts of the brain appear
to serve specific roles within the reading process.
This work comes from examining brain-damaged adults
who display highly specific abnormalities. For
instance, one category of patient can not read words
as a whole, but has to examine each individual
letter before concluding what the word might be.
Several investigators have recently suggested that
these specific impairments may be analogous to the
kinds of impairments in reading which poor readers
have. However, there is no strong experimental
evidence, as yet, to support this contention.

We have discussed reading difficulties so far
in terms of the impoverished development of
cognitive processes, possibly due to biological
immaturity. But the home environment also has a
role to play in the development of reading. So much
so, that any visitor to schools in poorer districts
will find a much higher incidence of reading
problems compared with more well-off districts.
Having noted this relationship, we are hard pressed
for an exact explanation why this should be the
case. It seems that the involvement of the parent

in the child's reading is a very important factor. One study has shown that if parents are involved with their children's reading, through a carefully controlled training program, this has a substantial effect on the progress of the children, compared with when the same programme is carried out within the school. Perhaps the overall effect of parents is mainly as a motivator to the child. Another possibility is that the language of the working class parent in the home may not be sufficiently rich to provide a stimulus to the necessary development of verbal processes. This argument is not a strong one and some have argued that the language used in some working class environments is in fact just as rich as in middle class ones.

Examining environmental effects is quite difficult in practice. Most studies have usually given parents questionnaires. But this relies on the interpretations of the parents. One problem I came across recently gathering data of this nature, was that the reports of the parents of poor readers were more suspect than those of parents of better readers. In this study by Peter Doyle and myself we gave the parents questionnaires about their attitudes to reading and estimates of the time they spent listening to their children reading. Within the questions we buried the items from a lie scale. These items include such questions as "I never tell lies" which virtually nobody would agree with unless they were "faking good" or were actually exceedingly virtuous! We found that the parents of the poor readers were faking good compared with the rest of the parents. This might suggest a disparity between what attention the parents of poor readers think they should give their children and the amount of time they actually give them.

Part of the aim of this book is to highlight the problems currently facing researchers within the field of reading. Reading research does not appear to be the kind of field that has produced any dramatic breakthroughs. On the other hand, in the last few years a lot of information has come to light on the reading process. One particular growth area has been the contribution of the relatively new science of Cognitive Psychology. This subject often emphasises the role of the component processes within dynamic systems. The nature of these processes can then be elucidated by careful experimentation. If the theory proves to be intractable to experimentation, it is not considered to be a scientific theory. The most frequently used paradigm to test out these theories has been that using response times and errors produced by subjects reacting to presented stimuli. The advent of the computer was the greatest catalyst for the development of this science. This initially provided an analogy in terms of the wiring (or hardware) which led to ideas such as short-term retention buffers being analogous to human short-term memory. Nowadays developments are concerned with such high-order computer programs as those controlling a robot or translating a visual scene. If we can specify the kinds of things a computer program has to go through in order to simulate mental activities that come naturally to humans, we might infer that similar processes are taking place inside our own heads. Many cognitive psychologists have now, as a result of these advances, turned to all kinds of practical applications and research in reading has been one of those areas which has benefited.

Chapter Two

DYSLEXIA AND INCIDENCE OF READING PROBLEMS

Before examining the problems of poor readers it
would be useful to specify more precisely the group
of children we are focussing on. As we mentioned
earlier, there is some controversy surrounding the
use of the term "dyslexia" as a term used to
describe a particular group of poor readers. We
will be examining a broader group of poor readers
than this, but let us first examine the term
dyslexia more closely.

1. WHAT IS DYSLEXIA?

A dyslexic child is generally regarded as a child
who has substantial difficulties in learning to
read, but does not have these difficulties in
reading because of his social background, problems
with hearing or eyesight or due to low intelligence.
In other words, a child is considered to be dyslexic
after possible causes of reading disability
involving his environment or obvious physical or
intellectual defects have been discounted.
        What tends to cause confusion about the term is
that a child may be a poor reader, but not be
classified as being dyslexic as such. In Britain,
for example, if one were to visit any primary school
which was mainly composed of children of parents of
low socio-economic status, there would probably be a
substantial number of children in that school who
could not read or only read a few words. But by the
way dyslexia is defined these children would not be
considered by researchers to be dyslexic. Instead,
they would be classified as retarded readers due to
a home environment which may be impoverished for a
variety of reasons. The parents may possibly be

unable to read very well, the language used in the home might be entirely different from that encountered in the child's reading primers, the parents may never be seen reading so there is no model for the child to imitate, and so on. By contrast, in a school servicing a middle-class catchment area, there will hardly be any child who will be unable to read; but those who are unable to read might well be classified as dyslexic, provided that in other respects, such as in intelligence, they are otherwise normal. Of course, amongst working-class children who are poor readers there will also be a much smaller proportion of children who to all intents and purposes will be dyslexic. If the "dyslexics" had been brought up in a better socio-economic environment, they would still be unable to read.

Many investigators are intent on keeping to the narrow definition of dyslexia as outlined and doing research into the causes of the problem. While it is very important from the view of making progress in the field always to use groups defined by exactly the same criteria, there are others who would argue that from a pragmatic viewpoint there are many more retarded readers (e.g. working-class children of normal intelligence with reading problems) who deserve to be studied as well (e.g. Benton, 1978; Rutter, 1978). Nevertheless, according to Pavlidis (1981), there is some recent evidence that the two groups (that is, dyslexics vs working-class retarded readers of roughly average intelligence) can be clearly differentiated experimentally in terms of the nature of their eye movements. However, Stanley, Smith and Howell (1983) failed to find a difference in eye movements between a group of dyslexics and a control group of normal readers matched on age and non-verbal intelligence.

If a researcher wants specifically a sample of dyslexic children, this is what he would do in practice (based on Vellutino, 1979). Teachers from a number of schools would be asked to supply names of any children who are severely retarded in reading. As a first step these children are given a reading test and those more than two years below their reading grade at school would be selected. For instance in the USA this would be done for children in grade 3 or higher (ie. 8 years old or over). For grade 2 children the criterion would be adjusted to be at least one year behind and first graders would not be used. Obviously, in grade 1 (6 to 7-year-olds) the children are only beginning to read so the apparent differences between individual readers will be relatively small and perhaps temporary. In a typical sample for grade 3, the average retarded reader would be equivalent in reading to normal children roughly two-thirds of the way through grade 1 and by grade 6 he or she would be equivalent to normal children roughly less than half way through grade 3.

The rest of the criteria are not based directly on reading performance. The children are then given the Wechsler Intelligence Scale for Children (WISC) devised by Wechsler (1949). This is the most commonly used intelligence test for children and is composed of a number of subtests. It has two main parts consisting of a verbal test and a performance or nonverbal test. Only those who have an intelligence quotient (IQ) over 90 (the average score of children taking into account their age is 100) on either the verbal or performance scale would qualify as dyslexic. Thus, children who are dyslexic have problems in reading on grounds other than those based on intelligence.

Other grounds for exclusion would be: problems in acuity of sight or hearing, problems of gross neurological and physical disabilities, maladjusted children (i.e. those with a behavioural disorder) and finally, children would be excluded who were attending schools not within a suburban or middle-class area. Having employed all these exclusionary criteria, the typical researcher is left with a residue of children who would be classified as "probably dyslexic". The general characteristics of this sample would probably be: that on average for every four boys in the sample there would only be one girl; they would have difficulties with such things as telling the time, naming the months and days of the week etc., perceiving spatial relationships including having difficulty distinguishing left from right; some might have minor signs of neurological impairment such as having abnormal reflexes (Vellutino, 1979).

Having given a generally accepted definition of dyslexia it is only fair to point out that the term itself is subject to much criticism. For instance, in the Bulletin of the British Psychological Society an article by Whittaker (1982), critical of the term "dyslexia" and calling those who used it "flat-earthers", provoked a flurry of subsequent correspondence ranging from the light-hearted to the

8

more serious. One correspondent wrote about the etymology of the actual word "dyslexia" as follows: 'The Greek roots are simply "dys" (="bad") and "lexis" (=word). Dyslexia is a bad word. That is all there is to it'. More seriously, Whittaker in her article condemned the labelling of a child as dyslexic on the grounds that it erroneously suggests that it is a medical condition. Therefore it would be the responsibility of the medical profession rather than of psychologists which in turn implies some form of medically-based treatment. She also discusses how various researchers have tried to widen the term to include deficits in such skills as arithmetic (Miles, 1978) and language skills (the World Federation of Neurology in 1968).

Certainly, dyslexic children have problems in these areas; for instance, Thomson and Grant (1979) noted that on the WISC subtest of Arithmetic, dyslexic children performed poorly relative to normal children. But it seems to make the term "dyslexic" rather loose if it includes children with deficits in other areas, if this implies that they need not necessarily be deficient in reading to be classified as dyslexic. However, one can sympathise with the view that each dyslexic child demonstrates deficiences in most but not necessarily all of a particular cluster of skills. The skill of reading is just one of the cluster of skills which are causing problems and is not necessarily the fundamental one from which the others emanate. Perhaps part of the motivation for such criticisms of dyslexia by Whittaker is that instead of pouring money into special clinics treating dyslexia, she considers that more resources should be made available for remedial help in State schools.

Similarly, the Advisory Committee on Handicapped Children produced a report (the Tizard Report, 1972) on children with specific reading difficulties. It argued that a danger was that the narrowness of the term "specific developmental dyslexia" meant that resources could concentrate on this relatively small group of children to the detriment of those with difficulties in other skills, but not classified as dyslexic. Instead they recommended that the term "specific reading difficulties" should be used for this small group of children and that the needs of these children should be catered for within the context of the general problem of reading retardation of whatever kind. In other words, remedial education, using remedial

9

teachers in each school, should be the vehicle with which to tackle the general problem of reading and the specific problem of those classified as having "specific reading difficulties". They recommended that in practice most retarded readers should receive remedial help within the context of the ordinary school, be it at primary or secondary level. Otherwise they could be deprived of contact with normal children, particularly as the general development of language is more likely to be stimulated in such a context, which in turn would enhance their reading. The Advisory Committee went on to acknowledge that "a very small proportion" of reading disadvantaged children with severe problems will need to be temporarily withdrawn from their regular school in order to attend a Remedial Education Centre.

Over a decade later it does not seem that the level of support for the backward reader is sufficient under the present financial stringency. One headmaster of a school I visited, which contained a special unit, recently claimed that he had only ten pounds for each child in his school for the whole year to cover all materials such as books, pens, paper, paints and so on. As we have seen, reading problems are most frequent in schools from working-class districts. Such schools are least able to use parent-teacher association funds to purchase more materials or to buy microprocessors and other teaching aid machines such as tape recorders and the like.

2. THE SIZE AND NATURE OF THE READING PROBLEM

The incidence of reading problems in primary schools is difficult to evaluate because it will depend on one's criterion of what constitutes a reading problem. Taken to an extreme, it can rightly be claimed that just under half of the population of school children are below average in reading, but the same could be said for the dimensions of intelligence, height, weight and so on. We could use as our criterion that the reader has to be dyslexic as previously defined; but as we have seen, this is rather a small and narrowly defined group within the much larger general group of children retarded in reading.

When discussing the prevalence of reading retardation in a country it is more usual to use a certain standard on a reading test as the criterion. Retarded readers would not be excluded on other grounds, such as intelligence, as in the case of defining dyslexics. One study has used a criterion that in order to be classified as having a major problem in reading, the reading age of the child had to be at least 2 years 4 months behind the average expected performance for children of that age (i.e. the age norm). This study took all the 9-, 10- and 11-year-old children living on the Isle of Wight, which has a similar social composition to the rest of England, and found that 6.6% of children were backward in their reading (Rutter, Tizard and Whitmore, 1970).

If intelligence is taken into account so that children were 2 years 4 months behind the level in reading expected for their age and intelligence, the incidence in the Isle of Wight study comes down to 3.7%. This second group of children were classified as being "reading retarded" as opposed to being "reading backward" because they were "retarded" in reading but not necessarily "backward" in terms of intelligence. In other words, the retarded readers are underachieving considering what one would expect for their level of attainment in reading. A further study of the same children two years later revealed that an additional half a per cent were reading retarded. The implication being that 4% of children have severe difficulties in learning to read. A delay of 2 years 4 months in reading is substantial in the context of a child aged 9 who had started learning to read only 4 years previously. Furthermore, children who for reasons of lack of intelligence, were unable to achieve an appropriate standard in reading are eliminated from this estimate.

There is some resistance to separating reading backwardness and reading retardation on empirical grounds. Curr and Hallworth (1965) carried out a large scale study involving two groups of 9- and 13-year-olds with over 700 children within each group. In order to work out reading retardation for each child, they first of all correlated reading level scores with nonverbal scores on the WISC. This subsequently enabled them to predict what the level of a child's reading should be, based on the nonverbal IQ score of that child. They performed a factor analysis on reading scores, reading retardation scores and many other measures of a psychological and social nature. Factor analysis is a means of determining major statistical groupings amongst the various measures being studied.

The major factor to emerge was one based on reading scores and nonverbal intelligence. This factor was identified as being connected with the concept of reading backwardness as there were also loadings above .3 on low social class, poor parental encouragement and so on. On the other hand, the reading retardation measures, based on how far behind subjects were in their reading considering their actual level of intelligence, came out as another important factor, but revealed no significant nor consistent loadings on the rest of the measures under scrutiny. They therefore concluded that the concept of reading retardation is of little validity as it was not connected with any of the measures that they had examined.

Standards of reading have apparently improved over the years. According to Start and Wells (1972), the proportion of 11-year-olds with a reading age between 7 to 9 years (in other words, children who are semi-literate) was 21% in 1948 compared with 15% in 1970. In the case of illiterate children (classified as below 7 years in reading age), there were 5% of these in 1948 and by 1970 it was down to 0.4%. Even in 1956 it was as low as 1%. However, this apparent improvement may have been due to the impoverished educational standards during the war or to the associated emotional factors due to the stress and upheaval of war conditions.

It is difficult making cross-cultural comparisons of reading disability because, as already seen, definitions of what constitutes reading disability vary across investigators. Also, even within a particular definition the criterion of severity is changeable. On top of all this, variations across countries can be for a variety of reasons. Ostensibly, the interest in differences between countries normally arises because of the differences in spelling systems or differences in education. However, the levels of educational resources vary according to how much each country can afford. There are also many other extraneous variables such as variability in the schooling of parents and the home background they can provide, variations in nutrition, general medical care and so on.

In the Unites States the incidence of reading disabilities, according to the National Advisory

Committee on Dyslexia and Related Disorders (1969) is 10 to 15% of school children. In Japan, the percentage of reading difficulty is reported to be quite low at only 1% (Makita, 1968). This low level may be due to parental involvement with the teaching of reading before the children start school, or else it may be due to their unique system of kana and kanji. Parents teach their pre-school children kana, which is highly regular so that each symbol represents a consonant-vowel syllable invariably pronounced only one way. The kanji, by contrast, are taught later and correspond to the Chinese ideographs representing whole words. Within the teaching of reading of English, it will be seen that children do much better if their parents are involved in teaching them to read and if they start off with a highly regular spelling system.

CHAPTER SUMMARY

The dyslexic child was described as a child with severe problems in reading, in fact such a child might be over two years behind in reading. The reading problem of the child categorized as "dyslexic" is not due to lack of intelligence, lower socio-economic status, problems with the senses, physical disability or maladjustment. This description of the term "dyslexia" has been criticised by others; for example, a point that has been made is that there is a cluster of symptoms which are associated with reading retardation. Thus, remedial resources should be applied to the larger set of children suffering from this broader spectrum of symptoms rather than to the smaller more narrowly defined group of dyslexics. The seriousness of the problem in reading in the UK is such that about 4% of children between 9 and 11 are likely to be about two years 4 months behind in reading age compared with the level expected for their chronological age and intelligence.

Cross-cultural comparisons are difficult because of variations in criteria across investigators and because of complications of orthographic systems, educational resources, levels of nutrition, and so on. It was noted that in the USA levels of reading difficulty are between 10 and 15% but in Japan the incidence of reading difficulty is quite low.

Chapter Three

TEACHING CHILDREN TO LEARN TO READ

It is a sad reflection on the current state of
reading research that this most crucial area, how to
help children with reading difficulties, has had the
least amount of research energy devoted to it,
compared with other areas of research into reading.
It is not difficult to see why. Assessing a
particular method of remedial teaching can be a long
thankless task stretching over months, perhaps
years. In order to do this effectively one has to
have the cooperation of teachers and headteachers
and to be able to sustain their interest. This can
be particularly difficult if some teachers are
assigned to control conditions in which the new
promising method of learning to read is not applied.
There is also a difficulty in terms of a variety of
factors which could affect the experimental results.
For example, there is variation across teachers in
terms of their effectiveness in teaching. There are
variations between schools as well as the host of
other factors which usually apply to reading
research: social class differences, differences in
intelligence and so on.
     In spite of the general lack of research effort
in the field, this has not restrained a multitude of
authors (including myself) from writing on the
subject. While many of their ideas for the teaching
of reading are imaginative and interesting, to my
mind they are of little use until the experimental
groundwork has been carried out. Otherwise, many
ideas could waste valuable teaching time. The main
reason for doing research into the remedies for
reading difficulties is that it should enable the
teacher to try out techniques which have been tested
and shown to be effective as well as point out
methods which are best avoided. It does not follow

14

that using one's common sense as a guide to the teaching of reading will prove to be the most effective route towards helping the child learning to read.

1. THE FIRST STAGES OF READING

Let us first examine what alternative approaches teachers have available when they start children along the road toward the mastery of reading. During this period the most widely used approach in the UK, North America and other English-speaking countries is to build up a set of words which can be recognized by the child. This is known as the "whole-word" or "sight-word" method of reading, as the child does not initially need to know that the individual letters composing the words represent individual sounds.

The whole word approach
Our spoken language is an almost continuous stream of sound with hardly any gaps of silence separating the individual words. To demonstrate this just tune into a foreign language radio station in a language with which you are unfamiliar. The stream of sound will seem almost continuous, and also appear to be spoken extremely rapidly. Now imagine that you are a young child trying to break these sounds into individual words. This will give some insight into the magnitude of the problem of understanding spoken language.
     When it comes to learning to read, the child gradually discovers that these word units are represented by clusters of symbols, with each cluster usually presented one at a time on a card. Not realizing that each letter symbol represents a unit of sound, the pattern of letters is learned wholistically as representing a particular word. Typically, the child is shown a "flash card" with a word on it and the child has to say what the word is. There is a danger at this initial stage that the child learns incidental marks on the cards, such as a stain or a tear, rather than the "squiggles" depicting the word. Before long most teachers start introducing exercises systematically showing that the letter symbols represent sounds. A phoneme is the sound, or sounds, represented by an individual letter. Each phoneme is dealt with in turn until

the child is able to make fairly automatic letter-to-sound conversions.

Many words have to be learned partly or wholly in terms of their visual appearance. One of the major reasons for using this whole-word approach is that so many words in English are irregular in spelling. For instance the word "dread" is pronounced "dred" even though the spelling "ea" is normally pronounced as a long-e sound as in "eat". The extent of this irregularity does not usually come to the attention of the fluent reader. In my own case the irregularity of our spelling system was brought home to me when learning shorthand, which represents the sounds of words, not their spellings.

The irregularity of our spelling system helps to preserve the etymology of the English language which originates from many sources such as Latin, Greek, French and German. Unlike most languages, English usually retains the spelling from the original language. The French, by contrast, regularly change the spellings of new foreign words to make them acceptable within the French spelling system. However, other countries have reformed their spelling more dramatically than this.

The rules of English spelling are actually very complicated and elaborate and certainly children find it very difficult to master all the subtleties. English spelling is constrained by the position within the word. For instance, the ie sound is usually represented by "y" at the end of the word (e.g. "try") and by "i" at the beginning and middle (e.g. "iron, climate"). The spelling of a word can also represent its grammatical structure, even though this spelling is not usually phonetically acceptable. For instance, "booked" would be spelled phonetically as "bookt" as the "e" is silent. Sometimes concessions are made: "learned" can be spelled (or spelt!) as "learnt", for example. It is unfortunate that the incidence of irregularly spelled words increases as a function of how frequently the words are used (e.g. "to", "of", "was" and "you" are irregular and highly frequent).

Returning to the rationale of the whole-word method, another major reason for encouraging the method is that it promotes reading for meaning at a very early stage. When a child has developed a small sight vocabulary, this vocabulary can then be deployed in various combinations to construct meaningful sentences. Gradually, new words are introduced in such a manner that the context clarifies their meaning. The pronunciation of the word would normally be given by the teacher who indicates, whenever possible, a similarity in spelling between the word to be read and a word already within the sight vocabulary. Developing a sight vocabulary is simply a matter of regular practice. Initially the child may be very slow at pronouncing the word, but reading speed will gradually improve. For those who are persistently slow, practice with flash cards on the more frequent words may improve their overall reading rate, as suggested by Harris and Sipay (1980).

The phonics method

This alternative approach, which is not used very much in the initial stages nowadays, starts with a limited set of letters which can then be built into many different combinations to make different kinds of words. Gradually more letters are added and then the children are given consonant blends (e.g. as in "trend"). As some words frequently occurring in the language keep recurring, the child also develops a "sight-vocabulary" during these early stages.

Perhaps in the end it really does not matter whether children are taught by phonics or by whole-word methods. Usually children will have to encounter both methods during their time learning to read, so the problem of which method to use could be regarded as simply a question of the order of encounter of each approach. But a serious problem could develop if either way of processing does not develop adequately. Most adults read mainly by reading words as whole units, but they do have the capability of slower letter-by-letter processing if necessary, especially when they need to read nonsense words.

A method of instruction which is half-way between the phonics and whole-word method is the "linguistic method". This involves the child encountering a limited set of words similar in spelling construction to form sentences (e.g. "A fat cat ran after a bad rat"). Bloomfield was an advocate of this method which was incorporated within reading primers constructed with Barnhart. The method is similar to the whole-word method in approach except that a phonics-type of decoding is also encouraged on the part of the reader. Typically, the words used in such primers are less frequently occurring words.

Reading styles

What differences in reading style emerge as a result of the experience of being taught by either the phonics or whole-word method? Barr (1974-75) examined the reading strategies of beginning readers (first graders), half of whom were taught by phonics and the other half by whole-word methods. There were 16 children in each group matched exactly for age and reading readiness before the teaching of reading began. They were tested in December and then again in May toward the end of their first year of learning to read. In the case of the whole-word group, although the children started with a restricted set of words, this soon developed into phonic instructions as well.

By December, the children taught by phonics had encountered three times as many words as those in the whole-word group. On the other hand, 90% of the words encountered by the phonics group were only three or four letters long, compared with a variety of lengths and orthographic patterns for the whole-word group.

A problem with testing children in such an experimental design is that when testing their level of reading, the results may depend on whether or not the children have encountered the words before. To allow for this problem, the children in both groups were given a test of words they had already encountered and a test of words with which they were mainly unfamiliar. It was decided beforehand what criterion would be used to classify each child as a phonic or a whole-word reader. A child would be classified as a phonics reader if one or more non-words were produced while reading; if the child gave an incorrect but real word he would be classified as a sight-word reader. Barr found that if a child was using a whole-word strategy and the word given was incorrect, 75% of these words came from words already within their sight vocabulary; for instance, one child said "come" instead of "rabbit" which had been encountered in previous reading by that child.

Using this classifactory system Barr found that there were 10 phonic and 15 whole-word readers from the phonic and whole-word groups, respectively, in December. By the following May these numbers changed to 13 and 14 out of 16, respectively. Thus initially the reading strategy was slightly more varied for the phonics group, but by the end of the year each group was using predominantly the strategy

taught in their particular class. The errors made
by children with a phonics strategy typically shared
two graphophonic elements (e.g. "bait" instead of
"bat"; "hot" instead of "hat"); this occurred in
58% of cases, whereas this occurred much less for
the whole-word children at 30% of the time. Thus it
is possible to teach either a letter-by-letter or
whole-word type of processing to children.

Biemiller (1970) observed the phases of reading
that children passed through in their first year of
learning to read. The 42 children in the study,
from two different classrooms, were regularly asked
to read aloud and their errors in reading were
noted. Biemiller argued that during this first year
there were three identifiable phases through which
most children passed. The middle phase was the
important phase which was defined as when the child
mainly made "non-response errors". Such errors were
committed when a child reading aloud stopped reading
when a particular word was encountered.

Throughout these phases, the children made
errors by substituting another word or non-word for
the word they were supposed to be reading. An
analysis of these errors revealed that there was a
slight increase across the three phases in the
percentage of errors which were words acceptably
within the context of what was being read. Words
which were considered contextually acceptable
occurred when the incorrect word made sense
grammatically and semantically in terms of the
context of the preceding text. Thus if the original
sentence had been "push the swing high" and the
child had said "wagon" instead of "swing", this
would still make a sensible sentence, even though a
new meaning was now given to the sentence. It would
be meaningful, for instance, to talk of a toy wagon
being pushed high up a slope. Similarly, if the
child adds new descriptive words which are in
keeping with the context (e.g. "the big swing"),
these would also be considered to be contextually
acceptable errors. If, by contrast, the child had
said "Push the going high", this would not be a
meaningful sentence.

Apart from this increase in contextually
acceptable errors there were other changes across
the phases. From the first to the second phases
there was a doubling of the percentage of errors in
which substitutions were made of words which were
graphically similar (e.g."house" might be read as
"horse"). This suggests that when the child enters

the second phase, much more use of graphic information is being made than before. In the third phase there was only a slight increase in the use of this graphic information; however, what differentiated the third phase from the other two was that the percentage of contextually acceptable words, expressed as a percentage of the words that were graphically similar to the required response, increased to over 70% in the third phase compared with just over 30% for the other two phases. The progress of the children was such that the majority of the children were in the first phase in October and about half way through the year there were roughly equal numbers within each phase; by the end of the year most were in the final phase with three of the poorest readers still in the first phase.

A clear explanation of these data is difficult as different analyses suggest slightly different interpretations. But it would seem that children in the first phase of reading acquire a limited sight vocabulary of words and when they encounter an unfamiliar word, they spontaneously guess what that word should be on the basis of the context of what has gone before. In the middle phase, by operational definition, they mainly stop when they encounter a word they do not know.

Biemiller suggests that in the mind of the child this is the beginning of the idea that a particular group of letters represents only one word. Reading speeds increased substantially through the three phases at 2.15, 1.57 and 1.18 seconds/word, repectively, when reading a simple 26-word passage. Thus the child in the middle phase is becoming more accomplished at deciphering the letters; but this is accompanied by an increase in producing words which are graphically similar to the words being read. As graphemic processing becomes more automatic, the child's resources can then return to processing the actual content of the passage. This information can provide a context which aids the identification of unfamiliar words, which is why in the third phase the child is committing more errors whereby words graphically and contextually suitable are substituted.

Biemiller argued on the basis of these findings that the use of contextual and picture cues in the teaching of reading as advocated by Chall (1967), for instance, may be distracting the child from the task which lies ahead, namely, to memorize the patterns of the letters representing the individual words. This advice needs to be qualified in that abstract words need to be presented within a context in order to identify their meaning. The first phase of reading is not really reading at all, according to Biemiller, as the child seems to be making more use of contextual rather than graphemic information. Consequently it is advisable to encourage children to move out of this phase as quickly as possible. In the study, as early as November nearly half the children were out of this first phase. Perhaps a concerted effort to get all the children out of this preliminary phase of reading as early as possible would go a long way towards eradicating longer term reading problems.

How initial reading is actually taught

When the child first arrives at infants school, as a rule he is not immediately given a reading primer. Instead he will mainly have play activities which are usually designed to improve the use of language and perceptual motor coordination. Stories are often read to the children in order to encourage language development and to cultivate a desire on the part of the child to want to discover what is within a book. This is further encouraged by showing attractive pictures illustrating the story.

At about the same time, some teachers give their children training in scanning from left to right, using simple dot patterns which the child has to tick at various intervals, or some other such task. Many children need to be actually taught that they will be expected to look from left to right across lines of text.

Written words are incipiently introduced, probably starting first of all with the name of the child written on his exercise book. The child begins to notice that parts of the classroom might have labels attached to them, such as the door or a window. In the exercise book of the child he is encouraged every day to draw a picture. Afterwards the teacher adds a label to the picture (e.g. "John's house"). Some time during this stage the first reading primer is introduced.

The teacher has well over 100 reading primers to choose from. For instance, "Janet and John" used to be a popular reading primer. It was first introduced in 1949 and is essentially a scheme which encourages the learning of whole words or "look and say". At the other end of the spectrum is the primer emphasizing the connection between individual letter symbols and the sounds they represent. For instance, "Royal Road" goes methodically through the individual phonemes before tackling a story. As mentioned before, the problem with the phonics approach is that we have an irregular spelling system. Consequently in any normal text read by the child there are violations of the letter-to-sound rules which have been learned. This is bound to make learning difficult. An imaginative way round the problem is the "initial teaching alphabet" (ita). This was a scheme invented by Sir James Pitman which applied letter-to-sound relationships much more consistently. It also used some symbols which are similar to letters in the English alphabet, in addition to the alphabet. The idea of the system is to start the child entirely on ita so that all words are regularly spelled. That is because each phoneme is always represented by the same symbol, no matter what the word. (Actually there are several exceptions in order to facilitate the eventual changeover to normal spelling. E.g. the k sound is represented by either "c" or "k" corresponding to where these letters occur in normal spelling.) This has a two-fold advantage. The child is able to learn to read much faster and the regular symbol-to-sound connections become well-learned. As far as the disadvantages are concerned, one is that after a while the child must transfer to normal spelling; thus the irregularities in normal spelling still have to be faced at some stage. Another problem is that even in a regular spelling system, symbols will represent different phonemes according to the dialect of the child. This is not too important, especially when the children are accustomed to listening to received pronunciation on the radio and television. A more important problem for children on the ita system arises when a child has to move away from the school in the middle of the scheme, because at present in the United Kingdom, for instance, there is only a one-in-ten chance that the new school will be using the ita scheme. Research has shown that ita children do learn to read very quickly, demonstrating the impediment in reading induced by our present reading system. However, there appears to be no significant difference in reading levels between ita children after they have successfully transferred to normal spelling and children on the more conventional schemes (Warburton and Southgate, 1969). Thus there appears to be little advantage to using the scheme, except that it does encourage children to read by getting them off to a flying start.

Perhaps this result is not too surprising. The ita scheme could be regarded as an extreme form of the phonics method in that there is an exceptionally long delay before a sight word vocabulary is encountered. Although not a true phonetic alphabet, it does give the impression to the child that our spelling system is highly regular. The child has got to master both methods of reading (phonics vs sight vocabulary) at some stage; but as already suggested, the order of encountering these methods or the emphasis put on each method does not appear to be important in determining the overall time it takes to reach an acceptable reading standard.

According to the Bullock Committee, which examined over 2000 schools, over 80% used at least two reading schemes when the children were 6 years old. Teachers tend to use both the whole word method and the phonics method to some degree in 96% of schools. Obviously there will be a considerable diversity as to what proportion of each method is taught to each child. This will probably even vary within each classroom, let alone across classrooms, that is if it is possible to quantify such proportions.

2. MORE ADVANCED READING

We have seen how in the first stage of reading the child becomes aware that the seemingly strange squiggles on the printed page which constitute letters are learned as clusters of letters with each cluster representing individual words. Later a letter-to-sound knowledge is built up so that new words which are acquired can be analyzed by examining in sequence their individual letters. Each or several letters are converted into individual phonemes, the phonemes are blended together and, hopefully, the blended phonemes can then be recognized as a word already existing within the child's knowledge of words (i.e. his internal dictionary).

All these processes are of no value unless in the end they result in the child understanding what he is reading instead of merely being able to pronounce the sounds of the words with which he is presented. This might appear to be an odd concept because surely if the child says the words, understanding of the word must also take place. But this need not be the case, especially when one hears the child articulate the words in an unemotional manner, devoid of knowledge of most of the content.

Perhaps reading at this point can be considered to be a skill very much at the cognitive stage. In other words the child is still consciously thinking about decoding individual letters, or trying to remember what a familiar pattern of letters of an irregularly spelled word represents. The child is devoting all his cognitive resources to this process. There is little spare capacity for the next stage which involves retaining sequences of words in memory, then combining the individual concepts of these entities into something which is meaningful. In this next stage of reading, the initial stage of recognizing words has now to be mastered to such an extent that decoding letters can proceed with some degree of automation. This should then make available sufficient capacity to enable higher level processing of the material being read. Thus the teacher has the two-pronged aim of first giving children continued practice at reading to make the initial stage of decoding more and more automatic and secondly giving encouragement to understand what is being read.

Crowder (1982) suggests that the eventual automaticity in identifying words that we achieve is well illustrated by the Stroop effect. This is a phenomenon reported by Stroop (1935) and occurs when subjects are given the name of a colour but written in an ink of a different colour. For instance, the word "green" might be written in red ink. In such circumstances, fluent readers take longer to read the word compared with when the words are not names of colours, but written in coloured ink. This effect is very strong as it persists even after extended practice. Thus it suggests a strong connection between the spelling pattern of the word and the actual meaning of the word. In the incongruent colours situation of the Stroop effect there is interference between the colour of the ink and the meaning extracted from the actual letters.

Reading comprehension ability
One way to examine the dichotomy between decoding words and higher-order processing is to compare

children who are either good or poor at reading comprehension, controlling for intelligence. Presumably, the good comprehenders have achieved the stage at which decoding is proceeding automatically, whereas the other group has not reached that stage, perhaps for a variety of reasons.

A problem with this approach is that most if not all reading comprehension tests are not good testing instruments. Tuinman (1973-74) examined five major such tests using altogether 1800 students. One-third of these were given the questions to answer by themselves without the benefit of having read the actual passage beforehand. The remaining students were given the questions after having read their accompanying passages. Those students not given the prior passages answered the questions correctly on average 32% to 50% of the time, when correcting for chance they should have only had 25% correct. This increase in performance is due mainly to the students using their general knowledge to answer the question. Admittedly for younger children this knowledge base will not be so large as for the students, so the enhancement in performance would not be so large. Nevertheless, it is an aspect of the test to be wary about. Also, variations in performance across experiments can be affected by small changes in administration, such as timing subjects (and making them aware that they are being timed) and whether the original passage is made available for consultation.

Golinkoff (1975-76), after reviewing studies examining differences between good and poor reading comprehenders, suggests that although there are problems highlighted by the Tuinman study, it need not follow that there will be a strong relationship between intelligence and performance on a reading comprehension test. Golinkoff describes the characteristics of the good comprehender as being good at word identification to the point of being automatic at decoding. Furthermore they are adaptable in their reading in terms of the pattern of their eye movements and the size of the units of text which are processed, and they are also adept at handling the concepts dealt with within the text. The poor comprehenders are described as being a less homogeneous group possibly falling into two categories.

Using my own category labels, there might be the low-verbal type who has a poor vocabulary and is generally poor on such verbal aspects as oral reading and comprehending text. This type may have poor word decoding skills as well. All the foregoing suggests a general verbal deficit which means that reading at a higher order is not yet able to take place. By contrast the second type, the poor integrator, has the capability for understanding the text and can decode the words reasonably well, but this type usually does not integrate the words together into meaningful text. However, if this integration is done for them to some extent, they can perform as well as good comprehenders. This result was obtained using college students (Cromer, 1970).

Further evidence for the poor-integrator category within poor comprehenders comes from recent work by Oakhill (1982, 1983). In one experiment (1982) 7- and 8-year-old children were carefully selected who were either slightly poor in their level of comprehension or quite skilled (7.3 vs 9.2 years in comprehension age). This selection was based on the Neale Analysis of Reading in which children are asked questions about a text which they had previously read out aloud. Both these groups were matched in terms of their accuracy in reading aloud the text which was subsequently tested. Their accuracy scores were about 8.5 years, which was good for their age. Thus the two groups differed in comprehension skill but were equivalent in the basic skill of identifying words correctly.

Oakhill then gave them a series of short stories, each consisting of three simple sentences and after a short pause they were given a series of test sentences. Some of these had been previously presented, some had information congruent with one of the stories and some were incongruent. Examples are shown below:

The plane flew over the house (original sentence)
The house was in Crawley (original sentence)
The plane flew over Crawley (semantically congruent)
The house was in a field (semantically incongruent)

The poor comprehenders had a pattern of results suggesting that they were worse at remembering the stories. They were more likely to identify the incongruent sentences incorrectly and correspondingly less likely to identify sentences incorrectly which could plausibly have occurred in a previous story. Thus the poor integrator has a problem in assimilating the information within a story.

This experiment might seem tautologous in that children selected as being poorer on one comprehension test turn out to be poorer in a similar kind of comprehension test. However the first test, the Neale, does not specifically test integrative processes. A general memory deficit explanation is not a plausible criticism of the experiment either, as although the skilled comprehenders remembered over 70% of the sentences compared to 60% for the poor comprehenders, this difference was not significant. ·

Oakhill (1983), in an experiment using very similar criterion groups of skilled and less-skilled comprehenders to her 1982 experiment, gave them a sequence of short sentences. After all the sentences were read aloud they were followed by cues which were either the general noun which had appeared in the original sentence or a specific noun which would fit within the context of the sentence. For instance, the sentence "The people built their houses out of ice" would be cued by either "people" (the original noun) or "eskimo", a particular noun within context. The task was to recall the sentence that was triggered by each cue. The ability to read a word which has a rather general meaning and infer a specific meaning according to the context is known as "instantiation". This experimental paradigm should be a good test of this facility.

The effect that was found was quite substantial. The memory for the sentences of the skilled comprehenders was greatly helped by the instantiated noun compared with being presented with the original noun (72% vs 46%). On the other hand the poor comprehenders were not affected by the type of cue, recalling 39% and 35% for the original and specific nouns, respectively. As in the previous experiment, there was no significant difference in the level of recall of the original nouns, between the skilled and less-skilled comprehenders, indicating reasonable equivalence in memory between the two groups.

The overall picture that emerges of the poor integrator, who by definition is a child of average reading skills but poor comprehension, is one in which there is a lack of assimilation of information given in stories; also, there seems to be no willingness to go beyond the information given. In the instantiation experiment, the poor integrators were poor at making inferences about the general nouns presented within sentences. In other words, they were not processing the information to a deep enough level. Other data of Oakhill's suggested that the poor comprehenders were capable of assigning appropriate meanings of general nouns to a specific context, even though the main experiment demonstrated that they chose not to use this skill.

Several studies have shown that poor reading comprehenders have poorer basic reading skills, although as we have seen, it is possible to select out children who are good readers but have poor reading comprehension. One instance of a study showing the relationship between comprehension and reading skill was carried out by Hogaboam and Perfetti (1978). In this experiment on nearly 70 readers aged 8 to 10 years, they found that the time it took poor comprehenders to read aloud a single word was much longer than for good comprehenders. For the younger half of the subjects, having to read aloud a word of two syllables resulted in the second syllable being pronounced a quarter of a second slower for the good readers, but over a second more for the poor comprehenders. For the older half of the subjects, the gap narrowed to a third of a second and 0.8 seconds, respectively. The same kind of difference emerged when words were compared with non-words. Although both categories of subject were unfamiliar with the non-words, these new words were decoded faster by the good comprehenders. The skills of the good comprehenders at decoding letters to phonemes were much more developed.

If poor readers have poor basic decoding skills this might well affect their ability to comprehend the materials. One would have thought that they would be less likely to use higher order semantic processes when given the opportunity. The evidence does not bear this out. Byrne and Shea (1979) gave second graders in Australia a continuous recognition memory task which involved being shown a series of words. By the end of the experiment each word had appeared twice and on the two successive occasions separated by a few intervening words. When each word was shown, the child should have responded that the words were "new" and "old" respectively. Some of the words presented on the second occasion were either semantically or phonetically similar to the original and should have been categorized as "new". For instance, if the original word had been "mule" the changed word, several items later, might have been "donkey" (semantically similar) or "jewel" (phonetically similar).

The poor readers had a strong tendency to choose semantically similar words, but chose phonetically similar ones infrequently (3.1 vs 0.7). By contrast, the good readers chose semantically similar words less often, but also chose phonetically similar words (2.1 vs 3.8). This experiment suggests that poor readers, because they are deficient in basic reading skills, rely quite heavily on higher order processing. It a·so shows that the good readers use phonetic codes while reading. This is further support for the penchant of good readers to process at the basic level of decoding.

Perfetti, Goldman and Hogaboam (1979) demonstrated that poor readers are more influenced by prior context when reading than good readers. Words were presented briefly under three conditions. In the first, the words were presented in isolation, in the second, within the context of unconnected words, and third, within the context of a preceding narrative. In this last condition subjects listened to a narrative. Each time it stopped a word was presented visually which was within the context of the narrative. For a proper comparison this last condition should be compared with the second, that is, within the context of unrelated words. All readers were fastest when given the prior context of a meaningful story, but the improvement in reaction time was by 30% for the poor readers compared with only 15% for the good readers. Thus the poor readers seem to make relatively better use of prior context. In absolute terms the good readers were still faster even when there was a prior context (665 msec vs 751 msec in reaction time). Without prior context the poor readers are very slow at identifying words, taking over a second to do so.

Present approaches to encouraging comprehension

While many children progress almost naturally from acquiring basic word decoding skills towards understanding text, others experience more difficulty. Durkin (1978-79) has studied in detail what teachers do at present to ameliorate this progression. Durkin's definition of how teachers

should promote the development of comprehension is
perhaps a strict one; this occurs when the child is
given help in understanding two or more words in the
text. Subsequently, the teacher may test the child
to see whether understanding has occurred. This
might be done, for instance, by asking for the
sequence in which various previously read events
took place. Durkin's definition does not include
the teaching of the sounds of the words. But it
does include explaining the meaning of single words,
as long as the meaning is explained in the context
of the sentence in which it occurs. Words vary in
their meaning according to the context of the words
within which they appear. Also, the same collection
of words can take on a different meaning according
to their positions relative to one another.

Perhaps a rather extreme illustration of this
point has been supplied by Sternberg (1977). The
position of the word "only" can change the meaning
of the following sentence in ten different ways
according to the ten possible positions it can
occupy: "Only I will treat the patient in my office
tomorrow". It can be seen that comprehension
depends on the ability to integrate the concepts
underlying words together in such a manner as to
understand the one particular nuance of meaning
represented by that unique configuration of words.
The teaching of this facility directly is what
Durkin considers to be the most effective method.

Durkin gives examples of such teaching. For
instance, a sentence such as "the little
kindergarten boy was crying" is written on the board
and the children say everything that it describes
about the boy. Each response is written up on the
board. Afterwards information <u>not</u> given about the
boy is asked for. Another exercise is to present
children with two sentences and ask if they are the
same. For instance:

He was killed by the train at the crossing
It was at the crossing that the train killed
him

The teacher might encourage the use of visual
imagery. For example, a paragraph describing a
person is read, imagined and then discussed with the
teacher. They might also discuss what details have
been omitted.

Asking questions about a paragraph can be a
useful exercise. Sometimes the questions may not be

answered on the basis of the information given. Another kind of exercise is the process of abstraction in which a paragraph with a few main ideas and surplus details has to be condensed by the child into a summary. The concepts of "main idea" and "supporting detail" can then be discussed.

In contrast to this approach is comprehension assessment, which Durkin feels is not particularly useful. In comprehension assessment, as the name implies, comprehension is assessed but no feedback is given about why an answer is right or wrong. In a study of 24 teachers of 10- and 11-year-olds Durkin found that actual comprehension instruction took place only 0.6% of the time, compared with 18% of the reading instruction time devoted to the less useful comprehension assessment.

One might think that perhaps the low percentage of time spent on comprehension instruction was because teachers were concentrating on teaching basic decoding skills. This was not so, as only 9% of the time was spent in teaching phonics, oral reading and word meanings, etc. About 21% of the teacher's time was spent in activities such as establishing order, doing nothing, marking without the child's presence, or changing from one activity to the next.

Durkin made several comments on other aspects of reading instruction. Reading primers are usually accompanied by manuals for the use of teachers. These manuals were primarily used by them in order to find out what likely new words wou` ̄ be encountered and to supply questions to ask on the basis of the story. The workbook and assignment sections of these manuals were used extensively throughout almost all the periods assigned for reading. Durkin considered such usage as indiscriminate, if not time wasting. It kept the children busy but did not necessarily improve their reading. Another difficulty generated by this volume of work was that there was a few days' delay between the child reading a story and being queried about it. Thus comprehension recall also became a matter of ability at remembering material and not just comprehension per se. The motivation for generating this large workload could be that it is one of the easier ways to teach and that is what is expected from parents. This kind of work was boring for the children and did not appear to be helping those who were poor readers.

Further aids to encouraging comprehension

One aid to comprehension in reading is visual imagery. The skilled reader, particularly when immersed in a novel, will often use visual imagery as a way of following the plot. If the reader happens to see the film of the book later on, the frequent complaint is that the characters were not like those imagined by the reader. The visualization element in readin⁻ at this level can be powerful. It might follow that encouraging children to use visual imagery at the comprehension stage could be very useful. However, experimental research has demonstrated that attempting to induce this strategy is not an easy task.

Anderson and Kulhavy (1972) had high school seniors read a passage of 2,000 words and found no difference in factual recall between those instructed to use visual imagery and controls. The problem was that over half the control group had also used imagery; conversely, one-third of the so-called imagery group had not followed instructions. The use of visual imagery was vindicated as those who reported using imagery actually learned more from the passage. Perhaps if the use of imagery had been explained more and if there had been more practice, a larger proportion of the imagery group would have followed instructions.

Other studies on the use of imagery as an aid to comprehension have shown that presenting illustrations along with the text can normally improve the memorability of the material, especially when the illustration is depicting spatial re ationships between described objects. Children can generate images but this appears to be related to their mental development. Perhaps this presents a "Catch-22" situation for the reading teacher: in order to help comprehension, the child can benefit from learning how to apply imagery. On the other hand, by the time the child has the capability of using imagery, he may already have developed the facility to comprehend the materials.

Another way of helping comprehension might be through the implications of schema theory (Askov, 1982). The idea of this partly derives from Bartlett (1932), who suggested that all our knowledge of the world is in some form of organization and has many connecting links. When we acquire new information this is interpreted and processed according to the schema (existing knowledge) that we already have. If we receive

infor ation at variance with our schema, either this
new information is adjusted to accommodate to our
schema or else the schema itself is adjusted.
The implication of this for teachers, according
to Askov, is that teachers need to be aware of the
likely schema that pupils already have. In the
early stages of reading primers the information is
usually highly familiar to the child. For instance
such primers often re`ate stories about the home
environment. When the child becomes a more fluent
reader, the textbooks are more concerned with
presenting new information, usually outside the
child's schema. Children who have a rich background
knowledge presumably would find it easier to
assimilate new information into their schema. Barr
(1982) suggests that the teacher should try to be
aware of the possible wide differences in schema
between pupils and match reading materials
accordingly. In addition, the teacher needs to give
the appropriate background material which may be
absent from the schema of many of the pupils.

3. IMPROVING THE MOTIVATION TO READ

We have seen from the work of Durkin that children
are presently given a tremendous amount of
repetitive work to `o while being taught to read.
Intuitively, this would not seem to be the right
approach; instead the materials being read should
excite the children's interest and curiosity to the
extent that it makes them want to read. All
children enjoy a good story and are curious to know
at each dramatic point what is going to happen next.
But children also vary, especially between the
sexes, as to what topics will interest them.
Schemes which are personalized to some extent can be
useful in this regard. At the initial stages of
reading the "Breakthrough to Literacy" scheme has
this aim. The child's own words are used as a basis
for the basic sight vocabulary within the scheme.
For one child it might even include words such as
"dinosaur", "prehistoric" and "Brontosaurus" and for
yet another it might be "spaceship", "lunar craft"
and so on.

Fostering an interest in reading
Interest in reading can be inculcated by the teacher
reading part of a story to the class and then

getting them to continue reading it for themselves in the book (Bamberger, 1976). Another way to promote interest is to have a large number of books available on different topics and for the teacher to encourage each child to read books close to his or her particular interests. Unfortunately, some research indicates that teachers are not particularly conversant with the current interests of their pupils.

Even children who are retarded in reading can excel themselves when they find material which they find interesting. Shnayer (1969) divided 484 11- and 12-year-olds into seven age groupings according to their reading level. Then they were all given stories at a level of difficulty which was two years harder than their measured reading age. The children were given a comprehension test and were also required to give a rating as to the interest-value of the story. Not surprisingly, children who rated the stories as more interesting tended to have better comprehension of the stories. But this effect gradually reduced as a function of the actual reading level of the children. Thus good readers were not so affected by the rated interest-value of the stories as the poor readers who had better comprehension when they were interested in the stories. Unfortunately, what tends to happen is that older children who are still retarded in reading are given material which is basic and of little interest to them, because the basic material was designed for much younger children. This study by Shnayer indicates that these older backward readers are particularly susceptible to the interest-value in stories. Therefore the teacher needs to try to find appropriate materials, should they be available.

Interest in reading need not be fostered just by the use of interesting materials. Harris and Sipay (1980) make several practical suggestions. The teacher should avoid monotony by dividing an hour-long training session into perhaps four or five different activities. The occasional surprise can be valuable. Continued activity on the same task could produce the build-up of "retroactive inhibition". This can be regarded as a label merely describing the reduction in performance which results from maintaining activity in the same task. It can be due to motivational factors or perhaps it is related to the nature of the memory process. Repetitive tasks can be transformed by making them into games. One such game often used by teachers is a magnet on a string used as a fishing rod which can pick up different word cards which have paper clips attached. Games involving timing the children can bring in a competitive element which can heighten interest. For example, the class could be split into two teams and the teacher's questions have to be answered in a round-robin fashion. A score is kept of the performance of each team.

Reinforcers

Another way of improving motivation is by the age-old technique of rewarding the child. These rewards are called "reinforcers" by psychologists and can be applied in a systematic fashion in order to encourage reading. The main reservation that has been expressed about this technique is that there is the danger that the child could become absorbed with these rewards for their own sake and fail to learn that there is an intrinsic reward in the reading process itself. Unfortunately, there has been no research to my knowledge, applying the reinforcement technique in the natural setting over a sufficiently long period of time to see if it can produce a long-term benefit in reading.

The kind of reward can take different forms. For instance, the child may be given a sweet (e.g. a Smartie) at various stages, or points are accrued and when there are enough, they can be exchanged for a secret surprise or the child is given approval by the teacher in the form of a star stuck into his book or a letter of approval might be sent to the parents. Reinforcers, which give an indication of progress, seem to be quite effective. According to Smith (1969), when the progress of one group of children was plotted on a chart for their performance on word recognition and comprehension, they were just as good as a group receiving money for reinforcement and better than another group getting rewarded by free time and the praise of the teacher.

A system in which stars, points, tokens or something similar are collected and then exchanged for something else is known as a "token reinforcement" system. Martin, Schwyhart and Wetzel (1973) applied such a system to three remedial reading classes consisting of 95 high school children and another three classes constituted controls which received no token reinforcements. In the experimental classes a chart depicted work performance and general behaviour and it also showed how many points could be gained for satisfactory performance. The points were entered by the teacher on a daily basis, but no points were ever subtracted. After six weeks, the rewards consisted of school-sponsored activities and a letter of commendation to the parents.

This regime proved to be effective in improving work productivity in that absenteeism, obstreperous behaviour and non-directed activity were all lower to a significant extent in the experimental group. Unfortunately, it did not lead to an improvement in terms of reading achievement.

It would seem that there is a need for rather more research in this area. Individuals vary in their susceptibility to reinforcement, but in practical terms it might be difficult for the teacher to discover which type of reinforcer will suit which child. There is the problem that the extrinsic reinforcers (such as giving sweets) can lose their effectiveness fairly rapidly if they are withdrawn. Perhaps if reinforcement is combined with the use of interesting materials this problem will not be so acute, as the intrinsic rewards of reading should take over. Where the results of reinforcement have rapidly extinguished this has occurred in settings where the materials used have been very simple, basic and perhaps uninteresting.

The use of charts to give an overall impression of improvement seems to be a useful device. Harris and Sipay (1980) suggest that poor readers would particularly benefit and suggest the following examples which require a separate chart for each child: the thermometer chart has cumulative results such as the number of words or stories read charted by means of the red moving up the centre of the thermometer; in the skyscraper chart a window is added on each completed unit and the race-track chart has the child's progress represented by a horse. A group chart would be the bar graph representing each child and the completion of a unit requires the child filling in a new block on his own bar graph. There are many variations on this theme which can be allied to the individual child's interests, such as in swimming, running, flying, going on a space journey and so on.

4.   ORGANIZATION OF TEACHING TO READ

A problem for teachers in primary schools is exactly what to do about children who are poor readers in terms of allocating available resources to those children. Remedial teachers are now available in many schools, but how can this resource be used most effectively? Some problems that spring to mind are: at what age should remediation begin? At what point should it stop? What criteria (such as reading ability and IQ) should be used for selection? What would be the best methods of teaching? For instance, should the present reading scheme that the child is on be continued? How often in the week should children have remedial reading? What is the optimum group size? I have seen remedial teachers having to operate at the back of a classroom while another lesson is taking place. This is inadequate when, as we will see, poor readers generally have poor phonemic analysis skills which are easily disrupted by distracting background noise. Thus there are a host of questions to be answered, but there is not a great deal in the way of solid research to answer these questions.

Which children need remedial help?
The lacuna of research is particularly evident when it comes to considering the question of which pupils to select for remediation and deciding the point when remedial help can finish. The common sense view would be that remedial teaching should be given to those children who need it. But even setting aside problems such as defining criteria for selection, in a poor district a large proportion of several classes within the same school may suffer from reading problems and the remedial help available may be inadequate. Retardation in reading will not be noticed in the first year as the level of performance of all children will be low with a sight vocabulary of very few words. So remedial teaching would only begin after about a year into the teaching of reading.

Harris and Sipay (1980) advise against setting a minimum requirement in intelligence for remedial teaching. This is mainly because the measured IQ is inaccurate at this level; in any case, there may be maturation to consider which means that the child may have the potential to learn sometime in the future. There is not much of a relationship between the measured intelligence of children at the beginning of remedial reading and subsequent reading performance (Chansky, 1963).

The problem of getting a reliable diagnosis

Recent research work would suggest that there are problems in making an accurate diagnosis for the selection of children for remedial reading. Furthermore, even in the remedial setting there seems to be little agreement amongst the experts as to what exactly an individual child's deficits are and what needs to be done in the future about that child.

Vinsonhaler et al. (1983) gave learning disability specialists and teachers four case studies based on the cases of real children. They took care to select the most senior reading specialists available who had all been practising for at least five years. Three of them had doctoral degrees. The information given to these specialists and teachers was as follows:

> Across all the cases, the problem represented included sight-word deficiences, inadequate structural and phonetic analysis skills, inadequate oral reading fluency, and poor comprehension. Across all the cases, information about the child's achievement level, family and academic background, cognitive ability, reading ability, classroom behavior, etc., were presented in a variety of formats including test scores, completed test booklets, audio tapes, and written comments. Each simulated case was kept in a large file box which included an inventory listing the information (cues) available.

Each of these cases was yoked to an additional case with slight changes made to it. This was so that the consistency of each expert could be examined by presenting him with these two cases at two separate points in the course of the study to see if the same comments were made again about the same kind of case. They had to write a diagnosis and an initial remedial plan and their language was then converted into a standard vocabulary (e.g. "problem with visual memory"). In one study of 8 clinicians, on only 20% of diagnostic statements did they make similar statements for the same case when considering each individual. The clinicians were in agreement with each other on only 10% of statements made about the same case. Further studies on teachers showed an even lower level of agreement between individuals for diagnosis and remediation. Vinsonhaler et al. contrast this very low level of agreement with that amongst medical practitioners; although even here agreement is not very high. For instance, according to one study diagnosis of pulmonary disease from x-ray photographs produces 80% agreement between two occasions when it is the same specialist and 70% agreement when it is a different specialist. Medical training is characterized by an organized body of knowledge, the systematic collection of clues and the supervision of diagnosis and treatment of thousands of cases. In the case of training in reading these characteristics are somewhat lacking. Reading research lacks a rigorous theoretical framework and does not have a great deal of good supporting empirical work. The collection of clues is very varied across practitioners and case-study experience is slight.

One way round this difficulty would be the use of computer-directed programs which when worked through by the teacher or reading specialist would aid diagnosis. Part of the programs might even be involved in applying certain tests to the children. Doctors are already using computers to aid their diagnosis, a similar approach would at least produce greater consistency. This in turn might allow a more accurate assessment to be made of remedial methods.

Increasing remedial resources

In many schools there are a large number of children who might benefit from remedial reading, but only one or two remedial teachers are available. A problem arising from this is that where such resources are much in demand, it is feasible only to have large groups of children within each remedial session. But as might be expected, groups of 4 to 8 readers is a good size, but smaller groupings produce even better results according to a review by Guthrie, Seifert and Kline (1978). This same review suggests that 50 instructional hours are needed for sustained progress. The remedial teacher needs to divide her children into similar ability groupings and take each group at least about two or three times a week, giving them each time a lesson lasting three-quarters of an hour.

The actual organization of the remedial teacher needs to be such that she can have access to files, possibly located in the school office. These would consist of a folder for each child giving details of tests in reading, spelling and intelligence as well as details of specific reading difficulties of each child. Other relevant details should be included, such as events at home which may be causing emotional disturbance. There needs to be a record of the current progress of the child, i.e. what has been taught and what needs to be taught in the future. This may take the form of standardized sheets which are ticked in the appropriate sections. The children are tested at appropriate intervals and these results are entered into their files. Abbreviations might be used liberally in order that the time spent in record keeping is kept to the minimum. A school microcomputer, now becoming available in most primary schools, would be very handy for record keeping, as it could structure the information in an easy to use form. The school secretary might be used to transfer information into the files. Each child needs an envelope, or perhaps a container housed within the remedial classroom, containing his personal kit, such as exercise books, work cards, progress charts and so on.

The resources for remedial teaching can be considerably expanded by the use of voluntary help, as long as that help is closely monitored by the remedial teacher. This help can come in the form of mothers from the school, housewives from the local community, old-age pensioners, unemployed fathers, and even the school caretaker. Several programmed tutoring systems are now available which give specific guidance on the teaching of reading. The use of voluntary help is already working well in the UK with the evening-based adult literacy scheme and voluntary schemes in primary schools are already under way in parts of the USA.

The idea of using voluntary help can be of use in other ways not directly connected with the teaching of reading. A problem for the older poor reader is that although academic subjects such as Art and Maths do not suffer (some poor readers actually excel at Maths), other subjects such as History and Geography are more problematic because they require the ability to read at a level beyond the poor reader. Voluntary help would be most useful here in order to tape record relevant passages so that the poor reader can keep up with the rest of the class. This obviously needs the cooperation of the class teachers who could also help by giving oral tests to these particular children. If the poor reader succeeds in other endeavours within the classroom, this will considerably help his self-esteem.

CHAPTER SUMMARY

The first stages of reading can normally be approached in two different ways. In the whole-word method the child builds up a basic sight vocabulary of words, which when used in different combinations enable him to construct his own sentences. In the phonics method the child is presented with a small set of regularly spelled words in such a manner that a knowledge of the connections between letters and their individual sounds is built up. Children can be taught by either method, but inevitably the alternative approach has to be used at some stage. Despite debates on the issue it does not seem to matter very much which method is used first. The ways in which children are taught and the main reading schemes were described.

The next stage in reading is that of comprehension. It is argued that the first stage involving the acquisition of basic reading skills has to be mastered to a certain level in order that resources can be made available for understanding fully what the text is about. Experimental work has shown that readers who perform poorly on comprehension tests of text that they have just read are also poorer than good comprehenders on tests of basic reading skills.

In the USA, and probably in the UK too, the teaching of reading at the more advanced stage is done too repetitively. Furthermore, there is very little teaching about the comprehension process itself, according to Durkin. Children can get through so-called comprehension tests simply by referring directly to the original wording in the text, instead of making inferences implied by the content. Ways of teaching comprehension were suggested including the use of visual imagery.

Promoting interest in reading is important, so the materials need to be interesting in their own right. This might mean encouraging children to read books on topics which cover their own specific interests. Activity within the classroom needs to be varied. Boring tasks can be converted into games. Progress charts of individual children can also help and token reinforcement systems might be experimented with. The problems of remedial teaching were also discussed. In particular, more remedial help could be mustered by the use of voluntary help from within the school or from the local community.

Chapter Four

COGNITIVE FACTORS BEHIND POOR READING

This chapter deals with the cognitive factors (such as in visual or verbal processing) which lie behind the difficulty that a child has with learning to read. However, when we examine a problem such as this we need to have an understanding of the difference between stating that a cognitive factor is associated or correlated with reading difficulties and stating that a particular factor is causing a reading difficulty.

A correlation is a statistical technique which shows the extent to which two measures are associated. For example, within a large group of people there is a tendency for taller people to be heavier. This relationship between height and weight has been calculated to be 0.60 in terms of a correlation coefficient. The correlation can vary between 1.00, at which point there is an exact association between two measures, to zero, indicating no relationship between two measures.

Suppose we had measured the weights and heights of ten people and found a correlation of 0.64 between these two measures. This would be "significant" in statistical terms which means that this correlation is calculated to be a result which would occur by chance only on 5% of occasions. Traditionally this 5% boundary is considered by scientists to be the limit of significance. Suppose the correlation had been 0.40; this would not have been statistically significant for ten people, but had 25 people been tested and this had produced a correlation of 0.40, this would have been significant at the 5% level. Consequently it helps to know how many people are involved in a test and the size of the correlation when discussing a significant correlation. It is possible to have a correlation as low as 0.20 come out as significant only because it is based on testing 100 people.

But having found a significant correlation between two measures, determining the causal relationship between the two can be a tricky business. For instance, it has been shown that over the years, the income of ministers of religion has increased and over the corresponding period the consumption of alcohol has similarly increased. Juxtaposing these two measures implies a causal relationship. But in this case it is likely that a third factor, the increase in standards of living over the years, has contributed to rises in both measures. Similarly, if a correlation has been found between (say) children's ability to break words into individual sounds and their ability in learning to read, one has to be careful about inferring that the poor segmentation ability of poor readers is causally determining their lack of progress in reading. Indeed, it may be that causality in this case is operating in the reverse direction. The process of learning to read may increase the child's awareness that words are composed of units of sound represented by different alphabetic symbols. Consequently, children who are good at segmenting words are also better readers.

So far we have considered the case in which two factors are associated; these factors can be symbolized by A and B, respectively. A may be instrumental in causing B or vice versa. Another possiblity is that another variable, C, causes A and B. In our example, the intelligence of the child, as measured by an intelligence test, might be determining the performance on the phonemic segmentation task and on reading. Thus, having found an association between two or more factors, one has to be most careful about making inferences of causality. There is no mathematical technique nor standard statistical test that can be appealed to as an arbitrator of causal possliblities. Inferring causality is a matter of sensible judgement, although statistical techniques such as path analysis can be a substantial aid.

Let us examine the cognitive factors which have been implicated in the child's ability to read. A cognitive factor is considered to be any factor involved with thought processes, usually independent of such factors as the emotions and motivation.

1. AUDITORY OR VERBAL PROCESSES

At some stage when learning to read a child should discover or be told that each word that is encountered represents a series of individual sounds and furthermore that each of these sounds is represented by a letter or combination of letters. The units of sound (e.g. "b") are referred to as phonemes and the letter or letter combinations (e.g. "ch") representing these phonemes, as graphemes. Some graphemes represent more than one phoneme. For instance, the grapheme a represents two different phonemes as in "bat" and "bate".

It may be the case that some children never discover that there are letter-to-sound correspondences and get by through the expedient of memorizing individual patterns of letters. For most children if they are going to be able to read by breaking down each word into its letter-to-sound constituents, they not only need to be able to perform this particular task, but they will also need to reconstitute the segments of sound into whole words (e.g. Gibson, 1970). Some would argue that in order for children to read by letter-to-sound correspondences, the individual cognitive skills involved in the task (such as being able to break words into phonemes) need to be mastered. Some such as Wallach and Wallach (1976) suggest that children who do not possess such skills can be taught them and thus the transition to reading is made correspondingly easier.

Reading ability and phonemic processing
Experimental work has already established an association between the ability to decompose words into their individual phonemes and reading ability so that a child who is a good reader usually is better at phonemic segmentation. In several studies the evidence for this relationship comes from comparing groups of good and poor readers on their ability at phonemic processing. For instance Fox and Routh (1980), in a study in the States of first grade children (aged 6 to 7 years), found that those of average reading ability or who had mild problems in reading could break syllables into their phonemic parts, but children with severe reading difficulty could not. Again, Zifcak (1981) in a study of first graders found a correlation of 0.69 between their ability at inventing spellings and their level of

reading and a correlation of 0.78 between their ability to break words into individual sounds and reading level.

As mentioned before, a problem with finding an association between phonemic processing and reading ability is that it may be that the experience of reading is responsible for enhancing phonemic processing. An alternative view would be that there is a cognitive subskill of phonemic segmentation, independent of reading performance, which possibly matures in time and which causally determines performance in reading.

A study by Bradley and Bryant (1978) carefully controlled for experience in reading while examining performance on phonemic processing. They had a group of remedial readers averaging 10 years of age and their comparison group were normal readers of the same reading age, but who were on average 3 years younger. The two groups were matched for intelligence (at 108 points, 8 points above average). Intelligence quotients allow for the differences in age, so in real terms the retarded readers would actually score better on an intelligence test, but this score would be adjusted to take into account their respective ages.

Bradley and Bryant found that in spite of a superiority in intelligence in real terms, the backward readers had much greater problems in phonemic processing. An example of one task was that the child had to select the odd word out of a set of four which had a phoneme changed for one particular position in the word (e.g. sun, see, sock, rag). The number of subjects making more than one error was over three times greater amongst the backward readers at the level of 85% of the group. It could be argued that as the reading level in the two groups was equated, the possibility of reading experience causally determining the level of phonemic processing performance is eliminated. This argument hinges on whether or not reading experience can be considered to be equated even though the level of reading performance is the same. Beech and Harding (1984) have not been able to replicate Bradley and Bryant's finding and in fact found the same level of phonemic processing performance between retarded readers and normal readers of the same reading age.

The longitudinal study is a good technique for determining causality as it can monitor changes in the child over the years. Presumably if there is an improvement in one skill, followed later by an improvement in another over time, this could be a good basis for inferring that the development of one skill is contingent on the development of another, provided that there is a reasonable theoretical justification as well. As with most experimental techniques the longitudinal study also has its faults. Among other problems it is cumbersome, uneconomical and there is a problem with giving the same participants the same test year after year.

A longitudinal study suggesting that an improvement in phonemic processing in turn improves reading has been carried out by Lundberg, Olofsson and Wall (1980). Using the statistical technique of path analysis they found that the abilities of their children in dividing words into phonemes and also in reversing phonemes when they were at kindergarten were the best determinants of reading and writing skills some time later in these children. Unfortunately the majority of the subjects were reading to a small extent when they were first tested. So the study does not unequivocally demonstrate that early phonemic processing determines later reading performance. Those children already making advances in reading at the first testing may have improved in their phonemic processing as a result of their reading experiences. Later on, their reading performance might still have been ahead of the rest. Hence the result obtained by Lundberg et al.

Would phonemic training help?
Suppose that there was evidence that a child's ability to segment phonemes directly influenced the level of reading in that child. It would follow that it could be very useful for teachers to train children in the art of breaking words down into their individual sounds. Neuman (1981) did such training in a programme involving many exercises developing phonemic analysis skills. For instance, the children were given exercises in recognizing the similarities and differences in the phonemes in the beginning, middle and ends of words. They also had to do exercises involving looking for words that rhymed. The experiment lasted over 8 months and involved 256 children at first grade level. Neuman found that phonemic processing in general significantly improved over the period and was significantly better than a control group not

receiving such instruction. The control group had been given a variety of activities such as reading, games of mathematics and art projects instead of instruction in phonemic processing. Neuman then went on to see if there had been an improvement in reading in the experimental group over the reading group. Unfortunately there was no significant difference between the experimental and control groups at the end of the training period and in fact the control group was slightly better in their improvement in reading over the period.

There is evidence that if children are selected who are retarded in phonemic processing at an early age, training can improve their subsequent reading. Bradley and Bryant (1982, 1983) have reported a longitudinal study in which they tested 400 children in phonemic awareness before they learned to read at the age of 4 and 5 years. The next year they selected 65 who were poor in phonemic awareness and divided them into two groups. Both groups then underwent a training programme for two years over 40 sessions at 15 minutes a session. One group of children was given phonemic awareness training which included giving pictures of familiar objects during their training which they had to categorize by the sounds of the name, e.g. "hat", "rat" and "cat" would be grouped together. The other group categorized the pictures into different classes, e.g. all animals would be put into one group.

By the end of the longitudinal study, three to four years after initial testing, the children given training in phonemic awareness were three to four months ahead in reading and spelling compared with the controls. Thus phonemic training appears to be useful for children who are at least in the bottom 15% in terms of phonemic awareness according to this study.

But the Neuman study suggests that such training could be wasteful on resources for normal children. However, this conclusion could be unjustified because the different results may be due to other differences between the two studies. Bradley and Bryant monitored reading performance over a longer period of time. It might be the case that had Neuman waited about three years, the experimental group may have been significantly better. But as there was no sign of even a slight improvement over the controls after one year, this would be doubtful. Another difference was that the training period of Bradley and Bryant took place

48

after the first year and lasted for two years. This
could have been the time when phonemic awareness
training would have been most useful for the reading
process, possibly at the time when children were
changing from whole word to phonic methods of
reading. A final possibility is that the control
group of Neuman's study was trained in reading which
was sufficient to bring them up to the level of the
experimental group. Thus there was no significant
improvement in the experimental group.

Other verbal skills

There are other aspects of auditory-verbal
processing which are associated with reading
problems, but they do not seem to be quite so
closely related to the reading process from a
theoretical standpoint. One of these is the child's
speech production. One would not normally think
that speech would be related to the reading process,
but there is evidence for such a connection. For
example, in the Isle of Wight study more of the
retarded readers between the age of 9 and 10 years
had problems of speech than normal readers, as
assessed by a structured interview. Another example
is from Clark (1970) who reported a study on 230
poor readers between 7 and 8 years of age and with a
reading quotient of 84 or less on the Schonell
Graded Word Reading Test (the average reader under
16 would have a quotient of 100 no matter what his
age). She found that 28% of the sample had some
form of speech defect as determined by positive
scores on two items on a 26-item questionnaire
designed by Rutter (1967).

Another aspect associated with reading problems
is the child's ability to differentiate the sounds
in a word. The Wepman Test (1958) investigates this
ability by two consecutive words being read to the
child and the task is to say whether or not they are
identical (e.g. shot-shop, fret-threat). As can be
seen from these examples only one phoneme out of
three is changed within a word. Although
extensively used, there is a problem of response
bias with the test in that out of 40 items, 30 of
the pairs require the child to say "different".
This leads to a tendency for the children to say
"same" more often than they should, thus making them
appear worse than they perhaps are according to
Vellutino, DeSetto and Steger (1972) . The usual
finding of studies comparing normal and backward

49

readers on the Wepman is that poor readers do worse than the good readers (e.g. Blank, 1968; Deutsch, 1964). This relationship is probably not due to problems with hearing acuity as there is generally no relationship between this and reading disability (e.g. Kennedy, 1942), although this possibility does deserve closer investigation.

One possible reason for the association between the Wepman and reading problems might be that another aspect of the test, apart from speech perception, is responsible for the relationship: for instance, the necessity of having to retain two words in short-term memory, or the process of making a comparison between the word pairs. Another explanation could be that the relationship may be actually due to genuine differences in speech perception. It might be that the retarded readers have a deficit in verbal processing generally and that speech perception processes are one component of this process.

The idea of a generalized deficit in verbal processing in backward readers could account for other relationships between reading ability and other forms of verbal processing. In the Isle of Wight study described earlier, children were given the Wechsler Intelligence Scale for Children and compared on their performance on the verbal and performance (non-verbal) forms of the WISC. Among the retarded readers there were significantly more children with lower verbal than performance IQs. Similarly, Warrington (1967) found that in a group of 76 retarded readers, significantly more than expected had a superiority in performance IQ over verbal IQ by 20 points. She concluded that some delay in the development of language was connected with reading impairment. Thus, although retarded readers were generally backward in verbal processing over a range of activities including speech, remembering sequences of numbers, etc., nevertheless, as far as other cognitive aspects involving nonverbal processes were concerned, the retarded readers were reasonably normal. However there are one or two aspects of nonverbal processes which may be below par for the retarded reader.

2. VISUAL PROCESSES

Benton (1962) gave an early review of the literature on reading retardation and perceptual processes and concluded that there was a good deal of inconsistency in the work up to this point. In spite of this, there was some evidence for an impairment in the perception of visual forms and sense of direction in young children with reading problems. But these problems seem to evaporate as these children get older. For example, Harris (1957) found that 38% of 7-year-olds with reading problems had difficulty sorting out their left from their right body parts. In a comparison group with no reading problems only 5% of them had such a problem. In the case of the older children the incidence of right-left orientation problems reduced to 10% and 6% for 8- and 9-year-olds, respectively. Benton suggested that visual and spatial factors may play a prominent role in the early years of reading, but that they can not be important for the vast majority of older children who have reading problems. In any case, the small proportion of these older children with such problems seem to have a variety of other cognitive problems which implies some more general dysfunction than a specific problem with reading.

Another interpretation might be that children with reading problems are developmentally behind their contemporaries in specific functions, for instance, in certain aspects of visual functioning; these specific functions will gradually mature. However it may not be the case that these particular deficits were specifically holding back the child. So even though there is an improvement in these facilities for some of the older children, they are still not sufficient to improve their reading. This interpretation contrasts with Benton's in that Benton was suggesting that visual and spatial processes were important determinants of reading in the early reader, whereas another possibility could be that they are actually epiphenomenal, that is, they could be a by-product of the general cognitive immaturity of the retarded reader.

Yet another interpretation of the visual-spatial deficits in reading disability has been forwarded by Vellutino (1977, 1979) who proposed that underlying the problems in visual disorder was a problem in verbal processing. Rather than difficulties being due to the processing of visual material per se, the retarded reader is having problems with forming relationships between visual and verbal entities. In other words, during the reading process the child has to learn to associate recurring combinations of letters (e.g. -tion) to their corresponding sounds. If there is a problem in processing these sounds, it follows that associating visual symbols to these sounds also constitutes a problem.

Vellutino went on to describe two studies by himself and his co-workers demonstrating that for the retarded readers, their visual perception of 3- and 4-letter words is as accurate as for normal children, but verbal coding can be poor. The task involved either writing the words for the visual condition, or naming the words in the verbal condition after the word has been presented visually. They found that there was no significant difference between the normal and retarded readers when copying the words but a significant difference when naming the words.

This evidence is not entirely convincing. First, as previously noted, retarded readers have a tendency to have speech problems, so the "verbal" deficit may not be due to poor initial verbal coding (e.g. the retrieval of verbal codes) but due to verbal output. Second, and more important, the similarity in visual processing between the two groups may have been due to the performance in both groups being too close to ceiling; for instance in the case of 4-letter words, Vellutino, Smith, Steger and Kaman (1975) found no significant difference between normal readers copying 98% of words correctly compared with 83% correctly for the poor readers.

The Bender-Gestalt test

A discussion of deficits in perception of retarded readers can not pass by without including a mention of Bender's (1938) Visual-Motor Gestalt Test. In this test the child has to copy out a series of simple geometrical forms, for instance, a row of dots, squiggly lines and so on. Figure 4.1 illustates the kind of reproductions that a child makes when performing the task. Bender demonstrated that the quality of these reproductions varied with age and from this work suggested that visual-motor functioning underwent a qualitative change, especially within the period when the child was learning to read (Bender, 1956).

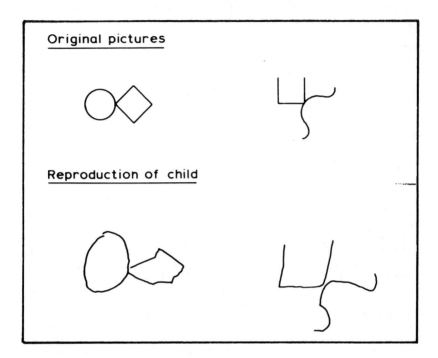

Figure 4.1. Two sample designs from the Bender-Gestalt Test and the reproductions of a boy aged 7:10 years with average intelligence and a reading age of 5:11 years.

Several studies have since found a significant relationship between reading problems and performance on Bender's test. For instance, de Hirsch, Jansky and Langford gave 37 tests to 53 children of average intelligence when they were at kindergarten prior to learning to read. When they were tested in their second grade (7 to 8 years of age) on reading and spelling, de Hirsch et al. found that reading in second grade was significantly correlated with Bender's test (r = .44) as administered in kindergarten. Children who were immature in perceptual-motor processing were also poor readers by second grade. Vellutino (1979), in evaluating this finding, points out that reading achievement demonstrated no significant association with another perceptual test (figure-ground perception), whereas reading achievement was significantly correlated with tests of intelligence ($r = .35$), behavioural stability ($r = .46$), "ego strength" ($r = .48$) and work attitude ($r = .43$). Thus the evidence that deficits in perceptual processing are connected with poor reading performance is somewhat equivocal.

The finding that Bender's test was significantly correlated with reading was replicated by Jansky and de Hirsch (1972) ($r = .41$) using a larger sample of 401 children drawn from a more diverse social background. In the de Hirsch et al. study, eleven children in the sample who were the poorest readers had problems of motivation. In a test requiring the accurate reproduction of pictures, such as Bender's Gestalt Test, it could be that motivational factors play a confounding role with reading achievement. Further support for this idea comes from a study by Lachmann (1960). A group of normal readers was compared with another group of normal readers, but who had been referred to a clinic because of emotional problems. A third group consisted of children referred to a clinic because of reading problems. All subjects were equated for sex, intelligence and age. The normal readers were found to be better than the other two groups on Bender's Gestalt Test. This suggests that perhaps the underlying factor producing an impairment on Bender's test may not be due to problems of a perceptual nature; instead it might be that in requiring children to draw out the diagrams this needs a certain degree of motivation. This would be lacking in the children with emotional problems, but similarly, there could be a lack of effort on the part of the retarded readers.

Another possible confounding factor to the significant relationship between reading and the Bender test could be that motor control rather than perceptual processing is impaired in the retarded reader. As the Bender test requires an element of motor coordination during the drawing stage compared with other visual tests, this might be why it is producing significant correlations with reading retardation in many studies. It might be noted that there is a multiple-choice test similar to the Bender test called the Beery-Buktenica "Developmental Test of Visual-Motor Integration" which does not require any drawing to be made. This test could be useful in removing this particular disadvantage. A final point to make about the Bender test is that there are other studies which have found no relation between performance on this test and reading retardation (e.g. Symmes and Rapoport, 1972).

Would training in visual perception help?

In the case of poor readers with problems in visual perception, if their poor reading is due to problems of this nature, training in visual perception ought to improve their reading. Research has shown that this is not the case. For instance, Rosen (1966, 1968) trained children in perceptual processing and improved their perception as measured objectively before and after training. But this did not improve their reading ability. Other experimenters have obtained similar results.

Bieger (1974) selected 54 children of poor perceptual abilities out of 108 second and third grade non-readers estimated to be of normal intelligence by their teachers (intelligence tests are not normally administered in some parts of the USA and could not be used in this particular study). Children with poor visual acuity were excluded. The testing that was used in order to decide which children had poor perceptual processing had the children identifying individual letters in lower case (e.g. "e"), undergoing a visual discrimination test for words and the Frostig perceptual test (Frostig, Maslow, Lefever and Whittlesley, 1964). Then the children were randomly assigned to experimental and control groups so that both groups ended up as equivalent on reading level and visual perception. Both groups were then given remedial instruction of one hour per week in reading; but in addition, the experimental group was given training in perceptual processing for 30 minutes during each of two one-hour sessions. Some subjects were actually taught for longer than this but this was counterbalanced across the two groups. A wide battery of exercises in visual-spatial processing was given including teaching figure-ground, perceptual constancy, spatial relations, sequential perceptual-motor exercises, shape completion, tracing forms and so on. The training began in October and in the following May 48 of the original 54 children were retested.

It was found that there was a significant

improvement for the experimental group on the Frostig perceptual test as a result of their perceptual training, but not for the control group. The test of the visual processing of letters and words was related more to the reading process than to the other perceptual tasks; it was found that both groups had improved in identifying individual letters but not in visually discriminating words. Similarly, both groups improved in their reading over 7 months with the experimental group gaining 6 months and the controls gaining 8 months in reading age. There was no significant difference in reading attainment between the two groups at the end of the training period. Thus children having difficulty in learning to read and who are poor in this ability to process visual information do not appear to benefit in their reading if they are given training in visual processing. Bieger (1978), in a study on 43 non-readers, obtained a similar result, again over 7 months. However, as we have seen from the Bradley and Bryant (1982) study, it is possible that the time at which cognitive skills training is applied could be crucial. Furthermore, it may be important to wait an appropriate length of time to see whether the training has taken effect.

There are a couple of other strands of evidence that perceptual processing is not crucially related to reading. First, Alexander and Money (1965) have noted that children with Turner's syndrome, which produces chronic visual-spatial problems, are usually normal readers. Second, Clark (1976) gave a number of tests to children who were good readers (over 7.5 years of reading age) when starting school. Despite being above average on tests involving verbal processing, these children did not do so well on a number of visual-motor tests using the Illinois Test of Psycholinguistic Abilities. Half of the children who had become fluent readers were at a lower level than expected for their age on visual processing. Put like this, this does not sound particularly remarkable; for any average group of readers, half of them would be expected to perform worse than the expected norm for their age. But the point is that some of these fluent readers were scoring 10 or more points below their own norm, which is considered to be a "substantial discrepancy" by Clark. Both these instances emphasize that an adequate level of perceptual processing does not seem to be a necessary condition for reading.

The stimulus equivalence problem

Blank (1978) suggests that while the simple perceptual-deficits model is certainly invalid, it may still be the case that normal reading needs a particular kind of visual information processing . During the course of such reading the child has to overcome the problem of stimulus equivalence. That is, the child has to make the generalization that a visual symbol representing a particular sound of a letter (e.g. "b"), although appearing in many forms, such as varying in size, colour or shape, still represents the sound of only one letter. Blank proposed that there are certain dimensions which have to be ignored by the child, such as those just mentioned, and the ability to suppress these irrelevant dimensions may be crucially important for the child learning to read.

In further support of this contention, Blank, Berenzweig and Bridger (1975) have found that poor readers do not seem to be very good at inhibiting these irrelevant dimensions. Instead they are distracted rather too easily and so find it more difficult to process through to the deeper level of what the visual symbols represent. This brings us back to the point that motivational factors could underlie those results, apparently demonstrating that poor readers have a particular deficiency in visual processing.

Individual differences in visual and verbal processing

It has been implied in the studies reviewed so far on visual and verbal deficits that children with reading problems may have problems in either of these areas. But it could be the case that some children have problems in visual perception, while others have problems in verbal processes and the rest have problems in both these areas or elsewhere. Several authors (e.g. Blank, 1978; Doehring, 1978) have been critical of the approach which classifies dyslexia as a unitary concept - in other words, an approach which considers the condition of being dyslexic as having the same range of symptoms for everyone under that particular title.

One of the best known advocates of this approach is Boder (1973). She categorized retarded readers into three separate groups on the basis of reading and spelling patterns. "Dyseidetic dyslexics" were considered to have visual perceptual problems and in particular in recognizing the whole visual pattern of the word. Another group was called "dysphonetic dyslexics" due to an inability to break words into individual sounds and to synthesize sounds into words and the third group was categorized as having both kinds of deficit. While not making a classification directly based on a verbal vs visual dichotomy, Boder's classification is based on a form of processing more directly related to the reading process.

There have been other investigators interested in individual differences in cognitive factors in children, such as Kinsbourne and Warrington (1966) and Myklebust and Johnson (1962). Mattis, French and Rappin (1975), in contrast to these investigators, used a brain-damaged control group of normal readers and their experimental groups consisted of brain-damaged and non-brain-damaged dyslexic children matched on age and intelligence. Brain damage was considered to be in evidence if there were mainly significant abnormalities on the electroencephalogram (which measures brain waves) or skull X-rays. On a battery of neuropsychological tests they found no difference between the brain-damaged and undamaged dyslexic children. Any cognitive deficits occurring in the brain-damaged readers which also occurred in the dyslexic groups were excluded as a cause of dyslexia.

Using a multivariate analysis, three separate clusters were produced with 90% of the 82 dyslexic children demonstrating one of the three following syndromes:

(a) Language disorder. The symptoms included problems in naming, comprehension ability, speech discrimination and imitative speech.

(b) Articulatory and graphomotor dyscoordination. On this dimension subjects were poor at sound blending and poor on a graphomotor test.

(c) Visual-spatial perceptual disorder. In this case verbal IQ was more than 10 points above performance IQ. Subjects were poor on a test of visual retention (Benton).

Their conclusion was that each of these three areas of cognitive functioning (i.e. language skills, motor-speech fluency and visual-spatial perception) were critical if the skill of reading was going to be mastered. That is, if a child had the kind of language disorder that they had found, for instance, this would preclude later reading.

But they have not demonstrated in their study such a tight causal connection. They would need to demonstrate satisfactorily the absence of these symptoms in normal readers. This criterion particularly applies to their third syndrome which has such few children in it that this could be a syndrome in which a similar proportion of children with this deficiency occur in the normal population of readers as well. Subsequent studies have cast doubt on the existence of this particular subtype. Furthermore, as we have already seen, visual training is not effective in producing improvements in reading for those children who previously had a visual deficit. Therefore this syndrome does not seem to indicate a promising area for remediation compared with the other subtypes.

Research into the various subtypes of retarded readers has used either clinical observation or some form of statistical clustering in order to derive its subtypes. According to Hicks and Spurgeon (1982) the results so far have been somewhat mixed; but probably this is because of such factors as a wide variation in the types of measures taken across each study and the variation in the types of subjects used.

In their own study, Hicks and Spurgeon examined 180 dyslexic children and 640 children referred to the University of Aston for clinical assessment due to reading problems. Factor analysis of the clinical group of poor readers produced an auditory subtype demonstrated by sound confusion, sound blending, bizarre spellings and so on. Another factor was considered to be representative of verbal labelling skills; this included phonic errors, left/right confusion and vocabulary problems. A similar pattern emerged for the non-clinical sample, except that the clinical sample had a more severe reading problem. Although certain visual measures emerged as important these could be accounted for in terms of verbal processing. For instance, in a visual memory task, ostensibly testing visual memory, it was conceivable that the poor readers had greater difficulty in labelling the pictures. There is evidence that poor readers between 7 and 12 years are slower and more error-prone than normal readers when required to name pictures of items (Denckla and Rudel, 1976).

3. MIXING VISUAL AND VERBAL PROCESSING

As part of the process of learning to read a child has to be able to transfer information from the visual to the verbal mode. For example, when reading aloud the child processes the print visually and then has to generate a verbal code to correspond with the text that is being read. We might suppose that this transfer across the modalities could be a source of difficulty for the retarded reader, and indeed this has generated a lot of research.

An interesting early experiment was carried out by Birch and Belmont (1964). In this experiment 9- and 10-year-old children consisting of 150 poor readers and 50 normal readers (balanced for age, sex and class) listened on each trial to the experimenter tapping a pattern on the table and then chose from three visually presented alternatives the correct pattern of dots. The interval between each pair of taps was either long or short and similarly, the distances between each pair of dots was either long or short. The maximum number presented was seven taps.

Birch and Belmont found that the poor readers were significantly worse on the task than the controls. Unusually, there was no difference between the two groups on the digit span subtest of the WISC; this involves finding the maximum number of digits that the child can repeat, forwards and backwards. They concluded, therefore, that poor memory for auditory sequences on the part of the poor readers, could not account for these findings.

Although these findings have been replicated several times, the study has been criticised on many counts. For instance, we mentioned earlier that reading for the beginner mainly involved translating visual input to verbal, whereas in the experiment the reverse was done, an auditory sequence was presented followed by the selection of the correct visual sequence. Actually, Beery (1967), performing the task using visual stimuli first, still found the same result. Another criticism is that in order to see if there were genuine difficulties in transferring across modalities, in this case from auditory to visual, a comparison needs to be made of auditory to auditory and visual to visual to see if these are correspondingly easier.

The most comprehensive study on this issue was conducted by Bryden (1972). Subjects were given sequences of auditory patterns, visual patterns or visual-spatial patterns. The visual patterns consisted of a light flashing on at various intervals. The three different kinds of sequences were presented in pairs of patterns on each trial producing all nine possible combinations, such as an auditory pattern followed by a visual pattern, and so on. The actual sequences were AA, VV, SS, AV, AS, SV, VA, SA, and VS where A, V and S stand for auditory, visual and spatial patterns, respectively. The task involved a group of retarded readers and a control group matched on age, sex and IQ who had to decide whether the pairs of patterns were the same or different. No matter the condition, the retarded readers were always worse than the normals. They were not especially bad matching across different modalities, the worst condition for the retarded readers relative to the normals being the matching of auditory patterns to auditory patterns. Thus there is no evidence from this experiment for retarded readers being particularly bad on tasks involving transferring information across modalities.

More generally, the experiments that we have examined briefly and many others including those examining the speed of shifting from one mode to another and those examining interhemispheric transfer have produced no conclusive evidence that there is a specific deficit in transferring between the modes for retarded readers. Some of these studies looked promising, but later more carefully controlled experimentation has cast serious doubt on the cross-modal deficit idea. A theoretical criticism by Bryant (1974) against the cross-modal explanation has been that in these experiments, such as those just described, it has been direct and easy to transfer from one mode to the another. For instance, a light coming on three times in quick succession can readily be compared with three clicking sounds occurring in quick succession. But in the actual reading task, the visual symbol representing the sound of a letter bears no direct relationship with the sound it represents. The closest letter bearing such a relationship is the letter "o" which resembles the appearance of the lips when the sound is made. But not by any stretch of the imagination can the nature of the sound be conceptualized as being circular, as represented by the symbol.

4. SERIAL ORDER PROCESSING

As mentioned previously, dyslexic children have difficulty in remembering the sequence of the days of the week, months of the year, and so on. This poor memory for sequences can extend to reversing two adjacent phonemes in a word when talking. It has been found in most experiments examining this issue that there is an apparent general problem with remembering the sequence of events in these children. Typically, in these experiments children are presented with a sequence of items and are required to recall them in the correct order. Under such circumstances retarded readers recall fewer items, whether the items are presented auditorily or visually. This does not conclusively suggest that retarded readers are just poor at remembering order, because if the order of recall is not scored, but simply the number of items correctly recalled, irrespective of order, retarded readers are still poorer than normal readers. So it might be that they simply have a poor memory for items of information, rather than problems in remembering the sequence of those items. Of course, it is difficult to sort out these two aspects of recall as remembering the order of the items also entails remembering the items themselves.

In an experiment on this question Hulme (1981) selected two groups of children with an average age of 10 with one of the groups two years behind the other in reading age but equated in IQ. Within each trial the children were presented with a series of six or eight letters which had to be recalled in the correct order. The method of scoring order was quite interesting as Hulme correlated the order in which items were recalled on each trial with the actual presented order. The advantages of this method are that if for instance two items are switched around in sequence during recall, some account is still taken of this; also, this method of taking the correlation is independent of the items recalled.

Hulme found that there was a tendency for the retarded readers to have a poorer memory for order than normal readers, but this turned out not to be significant. Hulme replicated the non-significant difference between the retarded readers and controls in subsequent experiments. This study is revealing in that it is probably the only one to date that has studied order memory independently of item memory and has demonstrated that retarded readers do not seem to be particularly impaired in their memory for order.

5. IMPLICATIONS FOR TEACHERS

As we have seen, cognitive factors such as visual and verbal processing are associated with reading failure, but it is difficult sorting out the cause-and-effect relationship between reading and these factors. If the relationship is a direct one, training children deficient in certain cognitive factors ought to help subsequent reading.

One study was examined which showed an improvement in reading as a result of cognitive skills training. It might be that previous studies showing a lack of effect of training have been applying training in skills at inappropriate stages during the reading process. Many educators (such as Harris, 1977) have proposed that the teacher should determine the skill weaknesses of each remedial reader, then take the child through a programme of mastering the skill in order that the reading performance might subsequently improve. While this approach seems sensible, it might be going too far at this stage to make overly specific recommendations as these may be costly in teaching resources. It would be useful to know, for instance, the point at which training on a deficit would be more likely to be effective.

Nevertheless, the evidence demonstrates quite clearly that reading retarded children do have deficiences in their language development. As this is a factor which interacts with social class, in that a higher proportion of children from families of lower socio-economic status have problems with reading, this might suggest that programmes in developing language, if successful, may improve reading ability. This has yet to be tested properly.

There are other aspects of cognitive functioning which have proved useful in the classroom, which have been examined in Chapter 3. One of these is the use of visual imagery in enhancing reading comprehension. Another technique which could prove useful in the future is that involving the tracing of letters.

The first proposal for the use of tracing in the teaching of reading came from Fernald and Keller

(1921). The technique involved the child tracing over a large word with his finger, the word having been previously written by the teacher in joined-up writing. Each segment of the word was spoken by the child as his finger traced over the relevant section; then the child had to write the word from memory. If there was an error the tracing procedure was repeated. The few studies on the effects of tracing on learning to read have generally produced favourable results, but they have been deficient in their research design. Hulme (1981), in reviewing studies on tracing, noted that tracing training in normal children, in contrast to retarded readers, does not seem to bring about any improvement in performance. Hulme himself conducted a series of experiments examining the effects of tracing on normal and retarded readers.

In the first experiment, the children were matched for chronological age and IQ, but the retarded readers were about 3 years behind in reading age. The children had to remember 6 or 8 consonants in the required order, either having to point to each letter or trace round it. Hulme found that tracing the letters significantly enhanced the subjects' memory for the letters, but this was significantly more so for the retarded readers than for the normal readers. For instance in one condition, retarded readers improved from 74% to 84% correct as a result of tracing compared with an improvement of 83% to 85% for the normal readers. A similar experiment was then undertaken using abstract forms, but this time the children were unable to name the items. Subsequent experiments produced similar results.

His conclusion from these experiments was that memory for letters was significantly enhanced by tracing only for the retarded readers, but both normal and retarded readers found the tracing of abstract forms to be helpful for a subsequent memory test. Furthermore, by using a control group of readers matched in reading age to the retarded readers, Hulme argued that the enhancing effects of tracing for the retarded readers was not a product of deficiencies in reading experience on the part of the retarded readers.

The use of the tracing technique appears to hold some promise for the future, but the appropriate experiments need to be done in the classroom to find out if the technique is worthwhile for the teaching of reading. Hulme's work suggests that it could be especially useful for the remedial readers, but perhaps less so for the normal reader. In spite of a lack of adequate experimentation the tracing technique is advocated by several present-day practitioners. The technique of tracing is often dubbed as "multisensory learning" because it is bringing further senses into the reading task: the ears (because the child hears the word he articulates), the speech organs and the tactual and kinaesthetic senses.

A recent study on multisensory learning by Hulme and Bradley (1984) might be noted in which they found substantial gains in 11-year-old retarded readers in a task involving learning the spelling of words. The method producing this gain in performance involved each word being shown to the child on a card. The word was read to the child who then repeated it. The child next wrote the word saying the name of each letter of the word at the same time as the child wrote the word. The word was repeated by the child once more. Finally, the whole process was repeated two more times. This mixture of all three modalities, visual, auditory and motor, in the learning of the task, was far more effective than only using visual-motor or visual-auditory modes, but only for the retarded readers. Normal readers, matched on reading age, but much younger chronologically (7-year-olds) did not benefit so dramatically by this method.

Augur (1982) has described her own teaching of reading as starting off remedial children with a limited set of letters (i, t, p, n and s) and using tracing as an integral part of her scheme. Each letter is on a card in the form of a block lower case letter and on the reverse is a picture clue to the letter (e.g. a picture of an indian for "i"). The card is in a transparent envelope and the child writes over the envelope with a felt tip pen the form of the letter using joined-up writing; at the same time the child says the letter. The five letters produce a large set of words including consonant blends (e.g. spit, stint, snip etc.) which are also traced and spoken in the same manner. Augur often writes the word on the blackboard and during the act of tracing the child wipes the chalk mark off the blackboard. Augur's technique is systematic in building up from well-established elements, that is, it starts from the five letters, builds these into syllables and words, introduces more letters and so on.

CHAPTER SUMMARY

We have examined cognitive factors associated with
reading retardation, starting with auditory or
verbal processes. There are clear associations
between reading retardation and skills such as the
ability of the child to break words into individual
sounds. The skill of the child in analyzing the
individual sounds in words was examined. It is not
yet clear whether training normal children in these
particular skills would transfer to their ability to
read. In one study there was no significant
difference between the children trained in phonemic
analysis and a control group of children with no
such training. But this was a short-term study.
Another study over a longer period involving
training in the second and third years was more
successful. This study showed that training
children who have a poor level of phonemic analysis
can be beneficial.

The idea that retarded readers have a
generalized deficit in verbal processing was mooted.
For instance on the WISC intelligence test a greater
proportion of retarded readers than normal readers
tend to have a better performance IQ (i.e. IQ
relating to visual-spatial processes etc.) than
verbal IQ. Although the evidence for the general
verbal deficit hypothesis is accumulating, there is
a need for experimental work in the classroom in
which children with such verbal deficits are given
verbal enhancement programmes to see if reading is
improved. It might be that higher-order language
training or a more general language training
(including speech training) may prove to be more
valuable.

Other aspects of cognitive processes relevant
to reading, such as visual processing ability, which
have provoked quite a lot of research were reviewed.
These nonverbal aspects have generally not been
found to be so important as verbal ones. One such
aspect was the ability of the retarded reader to
transfer visual information to its verbal or
auditory form. This transfer across the modes is a
necessary component of the reading process and early
evidence suggested that this could pose a specific
problem for the retarded reader. However, later
research and theoretical development rebutted this
evidence. Another area which initially held promise
was that concerning the dyslexic child's memory for
the sequences of items. Careful experimentation

66

distinguishing memory for items from the memory of the sequences of items revealed that although retarded readers have a poor memory for items, their memory for sequences is no worse than for normal readers.

There are certain aspects of cognitive processing which hold promise for the future from the point of view of the teaching of reading. One such technique is that involving retarded readers tracing letters and words with their fingers, while simultaneously saying the name of the items. This has been shown to facilitate their memory for the items. Interestingly, the technique does not seem to be so useful for the normal reader. This technique needs to be investigated further in a more natural setting to evaluate its usefulness more fully.

Chapter Five

DEVELOPMENTAL AND BIOLOGICAL
FACTORS BEHIND POOR READING

1. DEVELOPMENTAL CHANGES IN COGNITIVE PROCESSES

We are first going to examine the ways in which the
child changes over time both cognitively and in
terms of neurological processes within the brain.
These underlying changes could provide an important
clue as to why most children learn to read but
others do not. We shall see how important it is to
teach reading at the right time, when for various
reasons, the child can learn to read more easily.
Children vary in their rates of cognitive
development. It might be that the cognitive
processes underlying reading within children who are
poor readers may not have sufficiently matured.
Among other topics dealt with within this chapter,
reading problems in adults induced by neurological
damage will be examined, as well as neurological
correlates with reading retardation.

Early receptiveness to reading instruction
A commonly held belief is that children respond to
environmental stimulation much better while their
brains are maturing. Experimental work tends to
back up this suggestion of early plasticity of the
brain. For instance, brain damage early in life can
be compensated for much better than later on. This
generalization is no less true for reading, where
diagnosis in the first two grades, ages 6 to 8
years, can result in the remedial teaching of
reading being far more effective than later on in
grades 5 to 7, ages 10 to 12 years (Strag, 1972).

Muehl and Forrell (1973) investigated the effects of time of diagnosis on later reading by examining a group of children who had been referred to a reading clinic because of reading problems. These children had no signs of gross sensory nor neurological deficit. The effect of this diagnosis was to create the opportunity for many of the schools to give them special instruction and help. Five years later 43 of the subjects were followed up. When first diagnosed the children were retarded in reading by 3 years on average and on the follow-up reading were still found to be greatly retarded; only 4% had reading scores above average. Nearly all of them had IQs above 90, so intelligence was not an important factor influencing their reading problems.

Muehl and Forell found that clinical instruction given to some of the children had no significant effect on subsequent reading performance; however, the age when the diagnosis was made did have an effect on subsequent reading. The three levels of age examined were 9.1, 11.1 and 13.6 years and reading levels three years later were significantly correlated with age of diagnosis. The younger children in the study actually ended up with higher reading levels than the older children in the sample.

The diagnosis of these children in the study meant that the school was alerted to the problem; and in addition, the reading clinic to which they were referred could at that stage give specialist help. This included the provision of conditions in which the child could alter his self-concept. The parents were interviewed and told that their children had normal mental ability, but were just poor at reading. They were also persuaded that they should reward and encourage their children when they did well, but try not to be over-critical of them. The improvement in reading for the younger subjects as a result of this diagnosis may be partly due to the schools at the elementary level being better equipped, and perhaps more willing to give help. But the improvement could also be partly due to the developmental stage of these children. Perhaps they were at a stage when their reading performance could derive more benefit from more and better reading instruction than would be the case later on.

A cautionary note should be added in that Guthrie et al. (1978), in a review paper of various studies on remedial reading (mentioned in Chapter

3), found little difference in rates of reading improvement as a function of the age at which remediation began. But their comparisons were across different experimental studies when making comparisons across various ages at which remedial help started; this introduces a good deal of noise into the data. Also, it could be that it is the age when the child comes to school which might be the most appropriate point to begin remediation; and finally as Guthrie et al. point out, older disabled readers are much further behind their contemporaries than younger disabled readers. Therefore they require a longer period of time to catch up. Learning rates during remediation were quite high at roughly 2.5/year which is equivalent to a gain of two and a half years in reading for every year of remedial training at school.

The utility of screening

It could well be that children developing reading problems may benefit from early remedial help, although more experimental work is needed to see if this is so. Nevertheless, it follows that screening children, either before going to primary school or just on entry to school, could prove useful in alerting teachers as to which children may be in need of help in the future and what form of help would be best suited to each child. Screening is all very well in theory, but in practice it has not proved to be a perfect solution so far.

Silver (1978) outlines the requirements for screening the entire population:

Effective detection implies that the instrument can predict future reading failure; that the incidence of false positives is negligible and of false negatives minimal; that it can be given to large numbers of children quickly and economically; that the administration of the test and the interpretation of results can be done skillfully by school personnel after brief training; that the predictive instrument is able to locate those children who need more detailed and expensive diagnosis procedures; that it is statistically acceptable from standardization through interpretation; that it is appropriate for the population studied; that it provides a basis for intervention.

In laying down these rather tough, but highly desirable standards, Silver puts himself in a position in which all previous work can be dismissed as falling too far below what would be acceptable. For instance, he criticises the work of Satz and his co-workers, as reported for example by Satz, Taylor, Friel and Fletcher (1978). Satz et al. gave a battery of tests to nearly 500 children at kindergarten and examined their subsequent reading performance each year from first to fifth grade. Silver points out that although they had detected 58% of the severely retarded readers, the other side of the coin was that there were 42% not successfully identified.

A problem with screening is that there will be a proportion who will be predicted as being unable to read, but subsequently manage to read (false positives); and worse still, there will be children who are identified as being normal, but subsequently are shown to be poor readers (false negatives). At least some of the children classified as false negatives may have had the potential to be normal readers at the time of the screening tests, but they may have experienced some emotional disturbance which put their reading into jeopardy.

Present screening tests seem on the whole to be rough and ready. They are based on processes which investigators intuitively think ought to be related to reading performance. So skills in visual, verbal and cross-modal processing are tested as well as spatial, temporal and motor processes. As might be expected, predictions about subsequent reading performance from tests undertaken at kindergarten are initially more accurate than after a longer period of time. For instance, Satz et al. made correct predictions at the end of the first two years of schooling at 75%, but this fell to 57% by the time fifth grade was reached. On the other hand, perhaps we are expecting too much from screening. It ought to be regarded more as an iterative process, so that after, say, one year, the children are screened again and a re-evaluation is made. Thus the reduction in accuracy over a long period is not considered too deleterious in practical terms.

So far it has been argued that it might be easier to teach reading to a child with potential reading problems if that child had been spotted as a disabled reader earlier and had been given extra remedial help while learning to read.

71

Unfortunately, the prospects of correctly identifying such problems seem to be at the level of making a correct prediction perhaps for three children in every four, at least across the first two years of schooling. In one sense, this idea of catching children young to rectify developing problems runs counter to the notion that children with reading problems may have such problems due to immaturity in their cognitive processes. Crudely stated like this, it might suggest that one should wait until such children were more mature before teaching them how to read. Let us examine this theory in more detail.

Developmental lag in poor readers

Satz and his colleagues (especially Satz and Sparrow, 1970) have postulated that dyslexia is produced by a general maturational lag. Specifically, they suggest that from about 5 to 8 years of age children may be susceptible to perceptual and perceptual-motor deficiences in development. These particular skills develop quickly during this period within the normal child. However skills involving language and conceptual development are slower to mature and develop mainly within the age range 9 to 12 years. An underlying assumption of this model is that the child undergoes a set sequence of changes in cognitive processes. Each succeeding phase integrates and extends preceding phases in a way which produces an increasingly complicated structure.

Relating this concept to the beginning reader, when a child is not progressing at the normal rate during a period when particular skills are mainly developing, the child will experience problems in reading. This would be particularly the case during the period when the development of earlier skills such as visual perceptual and cross-modal sensory integration is progressing most rapidly. During this period the beginning reader is learning to distinguish the individual letters from one another. Satz et al. predict that eventually the immature beginning reader will pass through this phase of perceptual development. However, they will then also lag on the higher-order language skills which in turn further retards reading development. These higher-order skills will also be important for subsequent reading development as these will be required for such processes as understanding the meaning of connected discourse, predicting what comes next on the basis of the preceding context, and so on. Satz et al. are unsure if the retarded reader, aged 11 to 14 years, undergoing this higher order maturational lag will subsequently develop normally or whether this deficiency will remain for good.

In practice, testing this theory has proved difficult. Satz, Friel and Rudegeair (1974) carried a three-year follow-up of the cohort referred to earlier (Satz et al., 1978). Thus they could examine if the children predicted to be at risk at kindergarten, as shown by deficiences in certain cognitive-perceptual tasks, subsequently caught up with the rest of the children in the sample. The best predictors of subsequent reading failure at grade 2 were tests taken prior to learning to read on Finger Localization, Alphabet Recitation and Recognition Discrimination. They found no difference by grade 2 between the disabled readers and the rest of the cohort on the first two of these tests. This could have been due to both groups doing exceedingly well on these tests. At least we can conclude that by grade 2 the poor readers who were initially immature on these measures, subsequently improved on their abilities within these skills. If they had not all quite caught up in these skills by their second year of learning to read, at least they seemed to be very close to the rest of the children.

Vellutino (1979) is critical of this maturational lag theory on the grounds that there is the implication that at an earlier stage that there will be no difference between potential dyslexics and normal readers when they are younger on the higher-order processes involving language; and further, that such higher-order processing is unimportant for the process of learning to read. However, there is evidence that many children with early language deficiences become disabled readers. Furthermore, a good deal of quite sophisticated language development has taken place long before learning to read.

In criticizing Satz's maturational lag theory we should not throw out the baby with the bath water. Evidence is accumulating that poor readers are lagging behind in certain developmental features compared with normal readers of the same age. For instance, Harding (1983) found that although there were no differences in such gross physical features as height and weight between a group of retarded readers and a group of normal readers aged 7 and 8 years, reading retarded children had significantly less erupted secondary teeth incisors (p < .001). In common with other researchers, she also found that the retarded readers were behind on a battery of cognitive and perceptual tests. Beech and Kerr (in preparation) have recently found that boys immature in anterior teeth development were significantly behind in reading, but that there was no such relationship for girls. Factors such as visual and verbal intelligence and social class were controlled for in both studies.

The problem of sorting out precisely which immature processes in cognitive development relate to poor reading performance needs to be worked out more by experimentation than theoretical development at this stage. If developments in particular aspects of cognitive functions are the antecedents to the ability to learn to read, this would be very useful for the screening problem discussed previously. Thus children could be scanned for specific skills in which deficiences are good predictors of later reading ability.

Having stated that there is a need for more experimentation, the maturational lag concept also needs theoretical elaboration as it could take several different forms. This will be discussed further in the final chapter. Theorists have already mentioned the issue of whether a child undergoes a maturational lag in development or experiences a deficit from which he never recovers, thereby requiring more efficient areas of the brain to compensate. Another problem is that the child may be impaired in functioning at different levels for various subprocesses connected with the reading process. On the other hand, if a poor reader is compared with a younger child of the same reading age, it might be the case that the level of functioning of all subprocesses is approximately equivalent. It has to be remembered though that the older child, although matched on IQ performance, will be more intelligent in absolute terms. Thus, the poor reader can not be equivalent on all subprocesses with his reading age control.

Another issue concerns the problem of individual differences. It could be that a monolithic theory such as that proposed by Satz which states that most children with subsequent reading problems are immature in skills A, B, C, D, etc. during specific age ranges is not appropriate. Each poor reader could be immature in a specific configuration of skills, which if properly trained, would enable the child to begin reading adequately.

The term "maturational lag" implies a biological basis for retardation in certain processes. Beech and Harding (1984) propose the use of the term "developmental lag" to denote the more neutral concept of a lag which could be produced by both or either a genetically programmed development and/or environmentally influenced factors such as the experience produced by the language of the parents and teachers. If there is an environmental interaction with genetic predispositions to produce a specific level of cognitive development, this would imply that appropriate training in immature cognitive skills could bring cognitive development up to a level ready for reading processes to develop properly.

We have already examined a study by Bradley and Bryant (1982, 1983) which reports how this can be successfully accomplished when teaching phonemic awareness skills in children with severe problems in this particular area. The presence of a genetically determined maturational element would imply that there could be a level of cognitive development which is insufficient, even when the child is given ample training, to bring that child to a level at which he can successfully learn to read. Perhaps this consideration is a little academic as the training programs last for some considerable time (Bradley and Bryant's lasted two years), during which time a certain degree of genetically determined development would have transpired.

We are about to dip into the cause-and-effect problem again. Could it be that demonstrating that a poor reader is immature in certain processes could equally well imply that it is the process of learning to read which results in the good reader becoming more mature in certain ways? This notion can appear somewhat odd if it implied that learning to read enabled the faster eruption of secondary teeth incisors, as found by Harding (1983)!

Beech and Harding (1984) addressed this problem by testing a group of poor readers, a group of younger readers of the same reading level and a group of normal readers of the same chronological age as the backward readers. The two control groups were both matched to the poor readers on socio-economic status and nonverbal intelligence.

The retarded readers were on average 10 years of age
and had a reading age of seven and a half years.
The subjects were given tests involving phonemic
processing, such as rhyming tasks, a speech test and
so on.
     Beech and Harding found that the retarded
readers were significantly more immature in terms of
their ability to process phonemes, relative to
normal readers of the same age. But interestingly,
the level of this immaturity was not significantly
different from children of the same reading level as
the retarded readers, but roughly two and a half
years younger in chronological age than the retarded
readers. Beech and Harding argued that it was the
level of immaturity in phonemic processing that
could be determining the level of reading
performance. Of course, phonemic processing could
be part of a wider spectrum of cognitive processes
which were also immature, but the conclusion would
still be the same: that the level of cognitive
immaturity is determining the level of subsequent
reading performance.

2. READING FAILURE DUE TO NEUROLOGICAL DAMAGE

It should be useful to examine reading processes
from as many different approaches as possible. One
approach which may not at first seem relevant to
children who are poor readers, is to examine the
deficits in reading which occur in adults who have
lost their ability to read properly due to brain
damage. These were adults who originally had
learned to read, but as a result of brain damage to
part of the brain, lost the ability to do this
properly. These patients are usually referred to as
suffering from "alexia"; this term will be adopted
here in order to distinguish them from developmental
dyslexia, even though there has been a recent (and
in my view potentially confusing) trend to refer to
the alexias as the "acquired dyslexias". They have
been studied intensively by psychologists only in
the last few years and our knowledge about them has
come on in leaps and bounds. One thing that has
emerged is that they demonstrate strikingly distinct
patterns of deficit within each subgroup. This is
in contrast to dyslexic children who are difficult
to classify into various subsets, as we have seen.
When I state that they form distinctive groups, I do
not mean that the characteristics are entirely

homogeneous, but that the similarities between individuals within each group are quite close compared with the contrasts between these individuals and individuals within other subgroupings. Before proceeding it is important to note that these forthcoming comparisons between brain-damaged adults and children with reading difficulty do not imply that such children are brain-damaged. However, such comparisons are of considerable theoretical interest.

According to Patterson and Kay (1982) there are three central alexias: deep alexia, surface alexia and phonological alexia, and the more peripheral alexias are letter-by-letter reading, attentional alexia and alexia involving neglect. (As noted before, Patterson and Kay and other investigators use the term "dyslexia" instead of "alexia" as used here.) We will examine four of these alexias which are reviewed in more detail than here by Patterson (1981). Table 5.1 is a useful schematic representation of these alexias in terms of those dimensions which are important in distinguishing them and Figure 5.1 summarizes some major features.

Table 5.1. The presence (+) or absence (-) of a major influence of five word dimensions on oral reading performance in four varieties of acquired alexia. From Patterson (1981).

	Variety of alexia			
	Deep	Phono -log -ical	Letter -by- letter	Surf -ace
1. Word vs non-word	+	+	-	-
2. Content vs function	+	+	-	-
3. Concreteness	+	-	-	-
4. Word length	-	-	+	+
5. Spelling regularity	-	-	-	+

(a) Deep alexia

Perhaps the best way to conceptualize this syndrome is in terms of whole-word reading, sometimes more graphically referred to as "Chinese" reading. This latter term is used to emphasize that the style of reading involves processing the visual pattern of

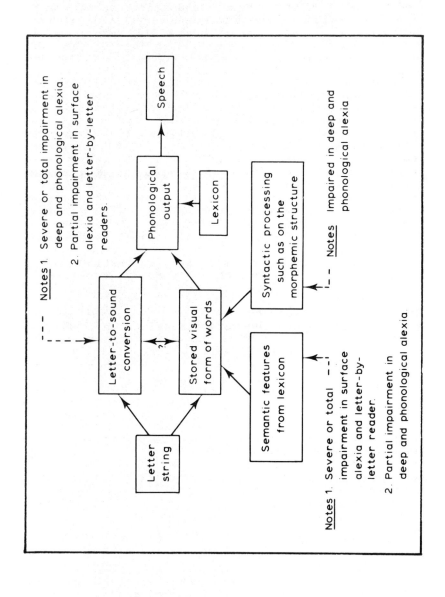

the whole words rather than decoding the individual letters into their corresponding sounds. The term "Chinese" is used because the Chinese system is logographic in that a Chinese representation of a word which is unknown to a Chinaman cannot be pronounced by him as the symbols contain no clue as to the pronunciation.

Deep alexics can not read non-words (e.g. "glink") as they can not be translated using letter-to-sound decoding. If pressed to make a response to a non-word, they might say a word which is visually similar (e.g. "glint" for glink). Deep alexics also have problems with abstract words (e.g."nice", "freedom", etc.) compared with concrete words. Related to this, content words (e.g. "map") are read rather more easily than function words (e.g. "and", "of" and "if"). In line with a Chinese style of reading, patients say words visually similar to the word given (e.g. batter is read as "butter"). Also, they make semantic errors such as "nephew" for "niece". The visual pattern of the word is evoking a word meaning close to that of the actual meaning of the word, but often the word is different in sound. Other reading errors made relate to a deficit in syntactic processing as just mentioned. Thus there are derivational errors (e.g. sign is read as "signal") and function word errors (e.g. a is read as "the").

(b) Phonological alexia
Patients in this category are very similar to the deep alexics. They also appear to be Chinese in their reading style, only more so, because in terms of reading words vs non-words, they read the words very well but are very impaired reading non-words. Two contrasts with deep alexics are that phonological alexics are not affected by word concreteness and do not make semantic errors. But, like the deep alexics they are affected badly when they have to read function words. A patient has been reported by Funnell (1983) who was like the phonological alexic, but was unaffected in his ability to read function words; so far, this patient is unique.

(c) Letter-by-letter reading
The first two described alexias involve a Chinese style of reading. The last two can be

conceptualized as using a predominantely but imperfect "Phonecian" style. This style involves translating individual letters into their sounds and working out what the word means on the basis of its phonological code. Thus the reader does not appear to have access to a store of visual patterns of words for which there are corresponding semantic representations in the internal dictionary. Letter-by-letter reading involves what its name implies. Patterson and Kay (1982) give the following description of the syndrome: (The patient) "identifies each letter of the word in succession, often but not invariably naming the letter aloud as it is identified. When he has reached the end (or nearly the end) of the sequence of letters, he produces the word". As might be expected, the time to read a single word increases monotonically as a function of word length. Interestingly, although reliant on identification of letters, the level of identification is not good, or at least varies in severity across patients with this syndrome, but patients are excellent at identifying digits which are logographic representations of words.

The letter-by-letter reader usually, but not always, is damaged in the occipital region of the left hemisphere (see Figures 5.3 and 5.4). This region prior to being damaged, along with its corresponding region in the right hemisphere, would have been involved in the higher-order processing of information from pathways from the eyes. The result of the damage is clear-cut in that the patient is blind in all the region of the visual field to the right of wherever he fixates. The patient is normal with respect to most other functions; for instance, writing proceeds effortlessly, but of course when reading it over afterwards, he is painfully slow. Another problem is that given a picture of an object or just a colour, the patient can have problems naming the object or colour.

(d) Surface alexia

This is sometimes called "semantic alexia". This syndrome can be distinguished from the others because the patient is sensitive to spelling regularity. In other words, irregular words are pronounced as they would normally sound if their spelling had been regular (e.g. broad is pronounced "brode"). The surface alexic patient of Marshall and Newcombe (1973) read out listen as "liston" and then said "That's the boxer"! As suggested before, this can be interpreted as a Phonecian style of reading in which the stored memory of a connection between the visual representation of the word and its semantic association is missing. Even so, there also appears to be some impairment in application of the letter-to-sound rules as well.

But Patterson (1981) suggests that instead of using letter-to-sound rules the same experimental results could alternatively be produced by the use of analogies, so that the word road would be identified within broad and hence produce the response "brode". However this analogical explanation, which relies on the Chinese approach to reading, does not really account for the increase in reaction times to read words as a function of the number of letters.

It might be noted that Marcel (1980) carefully examined the errors of surface alexics reading irregular words. For instance, barge was read as "bargain" and guest was read as "just". In these two cases the grapheme-to-phoneme correspondence rule is that e softens the g, but the rule was being applied in reverse here. So letter-to-sound rules were not being applied consistently. Marcel argued that other processes may be brought into play apart from letter-to-sound processes. However in my view there are no strong grounds for inferring any involvement of stored visual word forms.

Neither the surface alexics nor letter-by-letter readers seem to have problems with any of the dimensions affecting patients suffering from deep alexia and phonological alexia. They do not usually show impairments in the dimensions of words vs non-words, content vs function words and word concreteness. Thus they do not appear to have problems in letter-to-sound decoding, unlike the first two described alexias. Although the last two alexias can be viewed in terms of a Phonecian style of reading, it might be argued that the letter-by-letter reader does not entirely use this mode of analysis. Unlike the surface alexic there is no effect on spelling regularity, which would be expected from a completely Phonecian style of reading. Thus there may be access to a word-form system. But as there is a striking word length effect, this word-form system can not be operating in the normal manner. Perhaps in these patients the word-form system operates after letter-by-letter processing has been completed. But it does not operate by using analogies, otherwise more errors for irregular words would occur; instead, the correct visual form is retrieved. It might even be the case that phonological coding is unimportant, but that letter-by-letter processing is undergone without retrieving corresponding phonemes along the way. It might be possible to test for this experimentally.

Patterson's classification is by no means the only one. For instance, Benson (1981) has classified the alexias into three categories according to their neuroanatomical regions within the brain. Figure 5.2 illustrates the three sites of posterior, central and anterior alexia, respectively.

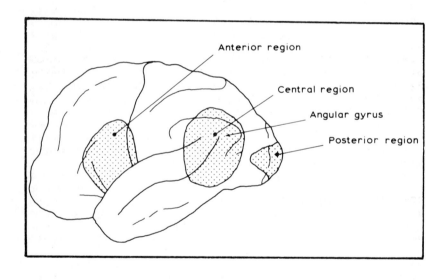

Figure 5.2. A side view of the left hemisphere indicating the three sites of three alexias, based on Benson (1981).

We are already familiar with posterior alexia because it corresponds approximately with letter-by-letter reading. A patient suffering from central alexia is totally impaired in his ability to read letters or words. Furthermore he has a severe impairment in his ability to read. Benson concludes that damage to the dominant parietal region, especially the dominant angular gyrus, produces this particular syndrome.

Anterior alexia has similarities with deep alexia in that it often occurs in lesions in the dominant frontal lobe. As in deep alexia, content words are read but not the function words. Furthermore, these patients can not name the individual letters in the word. These patients often can only write with their left hand, and even then, only with great difficulty. The written letters are badly formed and poorly spelled.

The adult alexias contain several theoretical implications for the study of reading. The deep and phonological alexic syndromes demonstrate that in adults at least, normal reading may proceed without the use of a process decoding individual letters into the sounds comprising each word. This is because the deep and phonological alexic patient can read normally even though the letter-to-sound processing facility is no longer available. These syndromes also suggest the separation of semantic and syntactic processes within the process of reading words because content words are read more easily than function words and root morphemes appear to be important in normal reading as these patients are poor at dealing with the affix; for instance, cast may be read as "casting".

The contribution of the letter-by-letter reading and surface alexias is that they illustrate how impoverished our reading is without the use of an intact word-form system which has direct connections with the internal dictionary. Nevertheless, there are times when a mode of processing involving letter-to-sound processing is useful; for instance, even without the benefit of reading Anthony Burgess's novel The Clockwork Orange we can read: "The gloopy malchicks scatted razdrazily to the mestro".

A contribution of the study of alexia, suggested by Marcel (1980), Holmes (1978) and others (as will be elaborated later) is that the reading errors produced are similar to those in beginning readers and some older children developing reading problems. Another implication of the work of adult alexics is that distinctive systems in the cortex function for specific purposes during reading. In particular, there seems to be a clear distinction between the processes of letter-to-sound processing and recognizing word-forms. It is possible that children experiencing difficulties in reading are immature within these areas of the brain in which these kind of systems reside. These areas might perhaps develop more fully at a later stage or else, because of some malfunction, processing has to take place in other areas, less well able to cope with these particular kinds of cognitive function. Unfortunately reading retarded children do not seem at the present time to divide so easily into such distinctive syndromes, but these latest research findings on the adult alexias do provide some interesting new insights for further research.

3. COMPARING DEVELOPMENTAL DYSLEXIA WITH ALEXIA

There has recently been an outbreak of papers making comparisons between the patterns of problems within developmental dyslexia and acquired alexia (Aaron, Baxter and Lucenti, 1980; Holmes, 1978; Jorm, 1979a, b; Marcel, 1980; Meudell, 1981; Wolf, 1982). We will examine in detail only the theory of Jorm who has argued that developmental dyslexia is produced by a deficit in the left inferior parietal lobule (see Figure 5.3) which Jorm suggested corresponds to the area of lesion in deep alexic patients. Warrington, Logue and Pratt (1971) studied three patients with an auditory memory problem for which they believed lesions in this region were responsible; but one of these patients actually had normal reading ability (Shallice and Warrington, 1975). The short-term memory problem of these patients along with other symptoms suggested to Jorm similar sorts of problems as those experienced by developmental dyslexics.

Both groups have difficulty in reading nonsense words, high imagery words are easier to read (Richardson 1975a, b) and visual errors are occasionally made in reading (Jorm, 1977; Shallice and Warrington, 1975). Furthermore, there has been evidence from studying the visual evoked potentials in dyslexics and normals that responses in the left parietal region differentiated the dyslexics from the normal readers (e.g. Preston, Guthrie, Kirsch,

Gertman and Childs, 1977). In this particular technique the investigator times the latency of response from the onset of a visual signal to the change in signal as detected by electrodes placed at specific locations on the head. Jorm also cited evidence by Lecours (1975) that the inferior

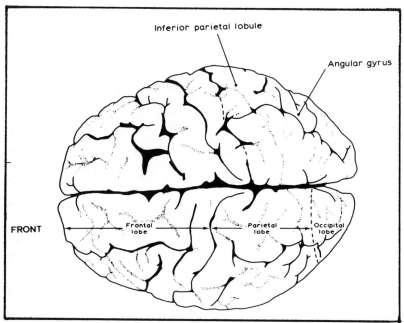

Figure 5.3. A view of the top of the brain indicating the positions of the inferior parietal lobule and angular gyrus as well as the locations of the frontal, parietal and occipital lobes, based on DeArmond, Fusco and Dewey (1976).

parietal lobes develop slowly and continue maturing through adolescence.

Jorm concluded that there are important implications for the teaching of dyslexics. If dyslexic children are similar to deep alexic patients, this implies that they can function adequately in terms of Chinese-like reading but are unable to make letter-to-sound translations. Therefore it would be best to ignore phonics methods of teaching and teach dyslexic children entirely by the look-and-say method. Another argument he brought forward was that because the dyslexic child is unable to use a letter-to-sound system, there are few opportunities to work out the word's identity. By contrast, normal readers have this facility and so can teach themselves reading to a certain extent.

Jorm's theory provoked criticisms from Ellis (1979), some of which were well-founded. Some of these criticisms were that there is inadequate evidence for an impairment in letter-to-sound translation in developmental dyslexics; that imageability of words affect normal readers just as much as dyslexics; that other forms of alexia may be affected by the imageability dimension; that evidence for a distinctive pattern of visual errors in deep alexia is weak, because it could occur elsewhere. Although Jorm made a rejoinder to these criticisms (Jorm, 1979b) there really is not a great deal of evidence available to test Jorm's theory adequately. Ellis notes the work of Holmes (1973 and 1978) which proposes that developmental dyslexia is like surface alexia; but again, the evidence provided by Holmes is equivocal, as shown by Jorm.

Baddeley, Lewis, Ellis and Miles (1982) have gone some way towards providing evidence relevant to this issue by examining whether dyslexic children have access to a phonological route while reading. They used as the basis for their experiments work by Patterson and Marcel (1971) which demonstrated that deep alexic patients did not seem to use phonological processing in a lexical decision task which involved deciding whether or not a string of 3- to 6-letter words were actual words (e.g. stane vs stain). Of course, although deep alexics can not read aloud nonwords, they can at least recognize nonwords as being nonwords on the basis of their own sight-word vocabularies. Also, they can repeat back the word if they hear it, so there is no problem at the articulatory stage. Patterson and Marcel tested whether phonological coding was involved in the lexical decision task by using nonwords which sounded like real words (these are called homophonic nonwords - e.g. stane) and nonwords which when sounded did not correspond to a real word (these are non-homophonic nonwords - e.g. dake). In normal subjects is has been shown that subjects are slower to judge homophonic nonwords than non-homophonic

ones (e.g. Rubinstein, Lewis and Rubinstein, 1971).
Thus normal subjects appear to use their
letter-to-sound coding facility during this
particular task, even though it is not really
necessary to carrying out the task. However,
Patterson and Marcel's two deep alexic patients
demonstrated no such effect and therefore probably
did not have this letter-to-sound facility available
to them. Baddeley et al. posed the question:
would the same lack of effect also occur in dyslexic
children, as suggested by Jorm's theory?

Baddeley et al. tested 15 dyslexic boys and 15
controls of the same age (about 13 years) and
intelligence. On average the dyslexics were 3 years
further behind on reading. Although the dyslexics
were slower than the normals on the lexical decision
task, they were just as affected by homophonic
words, indicating that they had access to a
letter-to-sound facility in the same manner as the
normals. This is in contrast to Patterson and
Marcel's deep alexic patients who showed no such
effect.

Baddeley et al. went on to test the effects of
word imageability on reading words aloud.
Interpretation turned out to be difficult because
the chronological age controls made so few errors
that the potential imageability effect although
significant was attenuated by a ceiling effect.
However a comparison between the dyslexics and a
group of reading-age control children demonstrated
that both groups were affected by word imageability.
This contrasts with Richardson (1976) who examined
dyslexics and found no significant effect of word
imageability on pronunciation latency and in the
lexical decision task. A contribution of this
particular finding is that the supposed imageability
effect in deep alexic patients may not actually be a
dimension pertinent solely to deep alexics.
Furthermore, as we shall see later, the imageability
effect is not consistently found in deep alexics
anyway.

Baddeley et al. concluded that unlike deep
alexic patients, dyslexics have a facility for
letter-to-sound translation although it was used
rather more slowly than comparable chronological or
reading-age controls. However, they concede that it
is still possible that dyslexics and deep alexics
are impaired in the same components of reading, but
an impairment during learning to read may have a
different effect on reading. Presumably they mean

that in the early stages of reading the brain may be sufficiently plastic to take on a limited form of letter-to-sound translation elsewhere in the cortex. Also, the programme of teaching at the school of these dyslexic children included phonics, whereas dyslexic children from another educational background may not have demonstrated any phonological coding in reading. Even though these findings of Baddeley et al. are a blow to Jorm's theory, it may be that dyslexic children have compensated for defective inferior parietal lobules by other less efficient parts of the brain being used instead. Unfortunately, this escape clause could ultimately render Jorm's theory untestable and unscientific.

4. HEMISPHERIC SPECIALIZATION

The differences between the hemispheres can provide insights into the reading process and difficulties in learning to read. The left and right hemispheres of the brain in broad terms are considered to be different from each other in that the left hemisphere is more specialized in processing language and is deficient in handling nonverbal information. There have been several ways in which this has been investigated. The right hemisphere controls the left hand; it is accessed by the pathways from the left visual field (that is, everything that can be seen to the left of wherever the eye fixates); similarly, it is accessed by the left ear. The left hemisphere has the opposite connections. The corpus collosum mediates between the two hemispheres so that information can be transferred across from one hemisphere to the other (see Figure 5.4). Some patients have had their corpus collosum removed in order to alleviate severe epileptic seizures. This has little apparent effect on their normal everyday functioning, but it has allowed the investigation of the separate properties of each hemisphere in the absence of the other. Similarly, investigators have examined patients who have damage to one or other of their hemispheres and found, for instance, that patients with left hemisphere lesions have problems in oral control and articulation (Bradshaw and Nettleton, 1981).
	Unfortunately, there are problems with much of the experimental work in that the investigated differences between the hemispheres may not be so

much a difference in processing but due to other factors. For instance, the right visual field is better at processing words, but this may be due to scanning mechanisms acquired through years of practising reading (Bradshaw, Bradley, Gates and Patterson, 1977). Again, there may be deficiencies

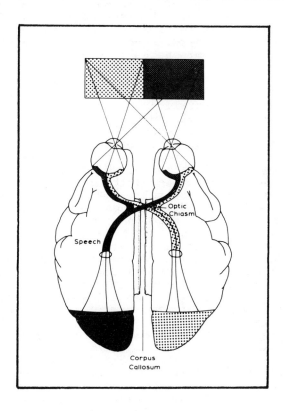

Figure 5.4. A horizontal cross-section of the brain at the level of the eyes looking from above. Suppose the subject is looking at the centre of the two boxes, information from the right-hand box would pass from the left-hand side of both retinas to the left-hand occipital lobe. Conversely, information to the left of fixation passes to the right hemisphere. The figure is based on Gazzaniga (1967).

in the way attention is allocated according to Kinsbourne (1970). It could also be the case that in normal subjects the longer time taken to process information in one hemisphere could be because the information is being transferred across the corpus collosum to the hemisphere better specialized at handling that type of information; rather than because that particular hemisphere is less efficient at processing that information but does not access the other hemisphere. However, the transfer time between the two hemispheres is probably too short to give a transfer time hypothesis much credibility (Swadlow, Geschwind and Waxman, 1979).

Bradshaw and Nettleton (1981) in their review of hemispheric specialization conclude that the left hemisphere is specialized for processing the order of events in time, the sequences in which items occur and the segmentation of stimuli. Evidence in favour of this is that the right ear is better at processing acoustic stimuli, which is rhythmical and complex, whereas the left ear is better for processing simple stimuli. The left hemisphere controls the limbs, hands and fingers when undergoing fast sequences in movement. Bradshaw and Nettleton also suggest that because of this facility of processing time and sequence in the left hemisphere, that it provides a basis for the development of verbal processing. If any advantage in the right hemisphere emerges this would be because of processing space within the left hemisphere being overcrowded.

Carmon (1981), in a commentary on Bradshaw and Nettleton's paper, provided interesting evidence to dovetail with their theory. Dyslexic children in several tests were found to have problems in the processing of temporal order, but their memory was good for visual patterns. Using a computer screen to display words, the individual letters were arranged spatially to spell one word (e.g. cat), but the order in which the letters appeared in these positions was that of a different word (e.g. act). Dyslexic children were better at perceiving the words, in terms of their spatial arrangement, than the normal readers. Carmon argued that as the dyslexics were deficient in temporal processing, the distracting temporal sequence was not such a distraction as for the normal children. This might very tentatively imply a left hemisphere impairment in processing temporal information for dyslexic children.

Deep alexia and the right hemisphere.
To return to the adult alexias discussed in the previous section, Coltheart (1980) and Saffran, Bogyo, Schwartz and Marin (1980) have suggested that the process of reading for the deep alexic involves mainly the right hemisphere. Deep alexics have substantial damage to the left hemisphere but no evidence of an impairment in the corpus collosum which connects the two hemispheres. Marin (1980) has mapped the areas of fairly extensive left hemisphere damage in five cases of deep alexic patients using head computed tomograms. A more simplified version of this is shown in Figure 5.5.

A word accessed in the right hemisphere for the deep alexic is processed from its visual form directly to a lexical-semantic system. This entails the activation of a set of semantic features specifying the meaning of the word within the right hemisphere. These then presumably transfer to the left hemisphere in order to articulate a response or to write down the word being read. It is less likely that the right hemisphere would be used for the purposes of output.

Further properties of the right hemisphere need to be specified to account for other features of reading by the deep alexic patient. The semantic reading errors can be explained in terms of the set of semantic features which are triggered, but are not sufficiently specific to retrieve the correct word. Consequently, words similar in meaning may be output instead. It is further argued that the right hemisphere is deficient in syntactic processing. Function words operate by their position in a context of words to indicate the semantic relationships between these words. As they do not have much meaning by themselves, but considerably add to the meaning of other words when they are in context, the right hemisphere can not translate these words. These aspects of the right hemisphere concur with other evidence concerning the nature of the right hemisphere (see a review by Lambert (1982), particularly in relation to the difficulty the right hemisphere has in phonological coding).

The connection between imageability and deep alexia is problematic, even though the right hemisphere seems to be better for visual imagery (e.g. Seamon and Gazzaniga, 1973). We have seen how Baddeley et al. demonstrated that imageability of reading words, controlling for word frequency, affects normal readers as well as younger readers

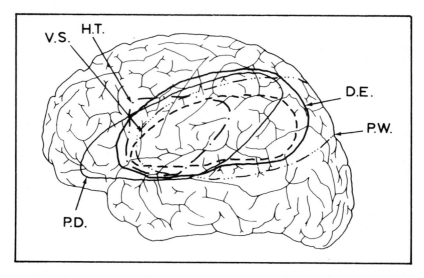

Figure 5.5. Composite pictures of the areas of damage of 5 patients suffering from deep alexia using head computed tomograms, based on Marin (1980), but simplified. This is a side view of the left hemisphere.

and dyslexics. The usual subdued effect of imageability in normal readers could be put down to a ceiling effect. In the past it had been considered that the imageability effect was a phenomenon confined to deep alexics, but this may be due to their poor level of performance. Furthermore some patients appear not to demonstrate the effect (Saffran et al., 1980; Patterson, 1979) and there is even one patient who demonstrates a marked effect in the opposite direction (Warrington, 1981). This deep alexic patient found it difficult to read high imagery words. Bradshaw and Nettleton point out that this patient (who died soon after being tested)

is unique; but it might be that there is some kind
of malfunction in the semantic features system which
affects concrete words but not other types of word.

Hemispheric differences between dyslexics and normals

Work on hemispheric differences between normal and
poor readers has generally revealed a right ear
advantage for both types of reader but an advantage
for linguistic stimuli (especially words) in the
right visual field for normal readers but not poor
readers. Usually the poor readers have no or
greatly reduced superiority in the right visual
field (Beaumont and Rugg, 1978). However Young and
Ellis (1981) argued that studies so far have had too
many methodological weaknesses for us to conclude
that poor readers have a different cerebral
organization from normal readers. For example,
there have been no studies in which poor readers are
compared with younger children of the same level of
reading ability. The process of reading at a higher
level may bias processing to be better in the right
visual field for the normal reader. Naylor (1980)
in another review comes to similar conclusions on
the basis of a wider range of techniques examining
laterality.

The issue of appropriate control groups brought
up by Young and Ellis touches on a point mentioned
earlier in the context of maturational lag. Young
and Ellis are implying that one would have to find a
difference between dyslexics and reading-age
controls in order to demonstrate that a difference
in hemispheric specialization is producing a problem
in reading. However, it could be that dyslexics are
maturationally behind normal readers of the same
age, but functionally equivalent to normal readers
who are much younger but of the same reading age.
Thus the maturational lag would be causing the
deficit in reading and also would be responsible for
the difference in hemispheric specialization. In a
situation like this there may be no difference
between dyslexics and reading age controls. But if
there was a difference between both groups and a
chronological age control group this would imply a
maturational change in laterality.

There are other avenues of study which get away
from the problem that the normal readers may simply
be more practised at reading, which produces
apparent differences between poor readers and

normals. Pirozzolo and Hansch (1982) have given a good review of these other research directions which include a description of two autopsies that have been carried out on poor readers. One was on a 12-year-old boy who had died as a result of a cerebellar hemorrhage (Drake, 1968). It was found that his gyri in both parietal lobes were unusually wide and the corpus collosum appeared to have deteriorated. The second case studied by Galaburda and Kemper (1979) involved a 20-year-old who was killed in an accident. He was left handed, had difficulty in reading and writing, a seizure disorder and an electroencephalography (EEG) abnormality.

In contrast to the previous case there were no apparent abnormalities of the cortical and sub-cortical areas and the corpus collosum was undamaged. However, microscopic examination revealed a degree of disintegration within the left hemisphere in the area indicated in Figure 5.6 which is mainly the temporo-parietal area, an important region for language. Abnormalities were particularly evident in the inferior parietal lobule and the angular gyrus; both these areas have been mentioned before. In normal people the planum temporale, within the temporo-parietal area, is larger on the left than on the right. But in this patient the planum temporale was the same size. Using computerized tomograms the left planum temporale has been implicated with dyslexia in a study of 24 dyslexics (aged 14 to 47 years) (Hier, LeMay, Rosenberger and Perlo, 1978). In ten of these dyslexics the right was larger than the left, rather than the other way round as in normal people. This suggests that a reversal in cerebral dominance seems to occur for some dyslexics, but not all. There was no evidence of brain damage from the computerized tomograms for any of the children.

Allen (1983) has recently argued that we should move towards examining hemispheric specialization in terms of smaller processing entities which he terms as "subprocessors". The problem then becomes identifying what a subprocessor does and identifying the location of the subprocessor within the brain. This means that cognitive tasks need to be subdivided into subprocesses, which is what is already being done in Cognitive Psychology. When it comes to examining the anatomical location of subprocessors, new techniques are emerging which could accurately locate these subprocesses.

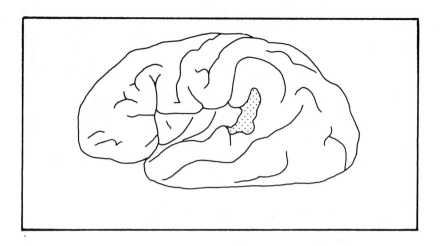

Figure 5.6. The dotted area indicates disintegration within the left hemisphere based on an autopsy of a 20-year-old who had been dyslexic. This view illustrates the side view of the left hemisphere, based on Galaburda (1982).

Allen lists three methods currently available going from the oldest to the newest: electroencephalography (EEG), event-related potentials (ERPs), regional cerebral blood flow (rCBF) and positron emission tomography (PET). EEG recordings involve measuring brainwaves. These are obtained by using highly sensitive electrodes which are stuck on the head by means of tape. The electrical activity picked up by these is monitored, amplified and recorded, usually by computer. The PET technique involves the use of radioactively labelled compounds which during the process of decay emit positrons. As a positron collides with an

electron it generates gamma rays and these are
monitored using a computerized tomogram. The
technique could be very useful for examining various
aspects of reading processes and relating these to
their corresponding locations within the cortex.
Unfortunately at the moment the PET method is
prohibitively expensive to use.

A new technique not mentioned by Allen, which
seems to be entirely safe, uses a magnetic scanner.
The patient lies inside the coil of a large magnet
which is switched on and off. This induces the
organs of the body to emit radio signals. These are
analyzed by computer to produce a map of a vertical
slice of the body (assuming the patient is
horizontal). The electromagnet has different
effects on hydrogen atoms within an ulcer or a
tumour and so on, compared with healthy organs;
thus the map reveals areas in which there are
problems. A recent development of this technique is
to use it to determine the chemistry of the brain.

5.   IMPLICATIONS FOR HELPING POOR READERS

The implications of developmental and biological
factors for helping poor readers are not so
immediately apparent as for the cognitive factors
reviewed in the last chapter. However there are
several practical implications from this chapter.

One of the first things we examined was the
notion of brain plasticity and the implication that
if reading failure was left undetected too long, it
was subsequently more difficult to get the child to
a satisfactory reading level. Some research
evidence was cited in support of this. Thus as
already advocated in Chapter 4 screening children
early, even as soon as they arrive in school, would
reduce reading failure. In parenthesis, it would be
very worthwhile if the remedial teacher within the
school performed this task. One problem might be
that in some schools covering poorer districts, they
might find potential problems in that screening
might elicit more children requiring remediation
than they have resources available to handle.
Nevertheless, I would like to see a large scale
longitudinal study in which children are screened
early and those children with potential problems are
given intensive remedial attention.

We have seen that if screening is done well
enough, three-quarters of the children who would

have had subsequent reading problems might be caught in time. Assuming that remediation is successful because it has been applied at the right time, this might leave about a quarter of that number two years later who might have reading problems. The remedial staff, as an ongoing process, could still cope with this smaller older remedial group as well as continuing intensive remedial teaching on the youngest children in the school. The comparison condition in this experiment would simulate the present situation in schools in which children are diagnosed rather later, when· there is concrete evidence that they are not keeping up with the rest of the class in terms of their reading.

It would be interesting to know from this experiment whether the first method in the long term is more efficient on remedial teaching time and, even more importantly, whether by the final year of primary school it produces far less poor readers. In order for it to work properly it would require well-qualified remedial teachers who were skilled at making diagnostic assessments.

The maturational lag theory that was reviewed has implications for the teaching of reading if one takes the view that maturational development might interact with environmental factors, so that a positive teaching environment enhances maturation. In the previous chapter it was suggested that disabled readers primarily suffer from verbal deficits in processing; training children deficient in these processes, especially in phonemic awareness, has been shown to be effective in helping subsequent reading, although the evidence is not strongly established as yet. A developmental lag explanation would be that perhaps such training was actually facilitating the growth of neuronal structures, or facilitating synaptic transmission, and so on in those areas necessary for reading development.

The work reviewed, drawing parallels between the adult alexias and developmental dyslexia, apart from telling us more about the reading process, could be useful in isolating processes which are problematic for dyslexics. For instance, Jorm's theory drawing these parallels was instrumental in producing the experiment by Baddeley et al. demonstrating that letter-to-sound processing was available to dyslexics. As this particular group of dyslexics had undergone a programme of phonics it might be that dyslexics do not normally have this facility; nevertheless, it does suggest that intensive teaching is worthwhile as it can make this decoding route available to them. Jorm argued that this facility enables a capability for the self-teaching of reading which should already be useful for children who make normal progress in reading.

CHAPTER SUMMARY

A crucial aspect of development within the brain is that learning to read can take place more easily earlier rather than later in the early school life of the child. It follows that screening children beforehand so as to catch those with potential reading problems would be very useful; instead of the widespread practice of waiting one or two years before beginning the remedial teaching of reading. There is a great need to refine present screening methods, but at the same time, they need to be in a form which can easily be applied and interpreted by school personnel.

Children who are behind their peers in reading development are also behind in other spheres of development, according to the maturational lag hypothesis of Satz. The normal child undergoes developmental changes in a particular sequence and at a particular rate, but the beginning reader has a slower rate of development in some functional aspects of cognition. Satz believed that early on the problem lies in perceptual and motor development, but by the 9- to 12-year age range, the primary developmental area shifts to language and conceptual development. The theory needs further refinement and experimentation, but it does look like a promising framework for subsequent research on the problems underlying poor reading.

The adult alexias were examined. Adult alexia is generally produced in adults when there is a failure in normal reading as the result of damage to the brain, such as from a stroke, a head injury, a surgical lesion and so on. Some different types of adult alexia were outlined which suggested at least two different types of reading skill. One skill involves the facility of reading individual letters, converting them to their corresponding sounds and identifying the words. The other skill relies more on using a knowledge of a stored set of word forms in order to recognise a word. There were allied impairments suggesting that word concreteness and the syntactic structure of the word (such as its morphemic root) are also important for the reading process. This work has already started to make a contribution to our knowledge of dyslexia, as it might suggest that dyslexics may have similar functional parts for the reading process which are underdeveloped or defective.

The differences between the two cerebral hemispheres were described. The left hemisphere is specialized for ordering the sequence of stimuli and for verbal processing among other things. The right hemisphere is more specialized for nonverbal processing such as spatial processing and music. The role of the right hemisphere for the adult reader was described in terms of the kind of processing taking place for the deep alexic who has substantial left hemisphere impairment and who consequently relies more on the right hemisphere. In the case of the comparisons between dyslexics and normals, work involving presenting material in the left vs right visual fields has not unequivocally differentiated the two groups as results seem to vary across studies. However, examinations of computerized tomograms have revealed abnormalities in the size of the left planum temporal in under half of a group of dyslexics, suggesting a reversal in cerebral dominance for these particular subjects. More advanced techniques of examining neurological functions which have been recently developed could be very useful in helping us identify different aspects of the reading process and relate these to specific subprocessors within the brain. Looking into the more distant future, such techniques might prove to be the most reliable in the screening of young children with potential reading problems.

Chapter Six

ENVIRONMENTAL FACTORS BEHIND POOR READING

It has already been mentioned that the socio-economic status of the child has a bearing on his ability to read and write. This is why the definition of dyslexia excludes working-class children. The working-class environment is acknowledged as having a detrimental effect on a child's endeavours to read. Not all working-class environments have a retarding effect, but the incidence of poor reading is very much related to class.

For instance, Morris (1966) sampled 100 good and 100 poor readers from five English schools within areas of either high or low socio-economic status. She found that 80% of the fathers of the poor readers were manual workers whereas only 27% of the fathers of the good readers were in this category. Likewise in America, Barton (1963) on the basis of 1500 classrooms concluded that by the beginning of second grade, upper-middle-class children were one year ahead in reading; whereas by the grades 4 and 5 lower-working-class children were a year or more behind in reading.

Why should there be this relationship? The answer is not so straightforward; it might even be mistaken to think that it is actually social class which is underlying the problem. For instance, it might be that parental attitudes, which are indirectly related to class, are crucial. Furthermore, although this chapter is mainly about environmental influences, there could be a genetic influence underlying this relationship between social class and reading ability.

1. PARENTAL INFLUENCES ON READING DEVELOPMENT

Miller (1970) gave 10- and 11-year-old English school children a detailed questionnaire and obtained a measure of their academic attainment on Verbal, English and Arithmetic scores as well as their social class based on parental occupation. A factor analysis of these data based on 489 children produced many factors, so only four are selected here which had the highest association with the achievement score.

Starting with those most strongly associated with achievement (correlations are shown in brackets), if parents were overly dominant and the child too submissive, this produced lower achievement ($r = .52$); if the child favoured intellectual enterprise, for instance, preferring an intellectual rather than a manual job ($r = .45$), this produced higher achievement; but achievement was lower if there was deprivation, that is, if the child felt rejection at the cultural, intellectual, social or emotional level ($r = .44$); and the fourth factor represented when the child was allowed a certain amount of freedom of action by the parent ($r = .35$). These same four factors correlated with social class at .23, .11, .20 and .15, respectively. Thus although there was a tendency for the middle-classes to be different from the working-classes on these factors, this was only a weak tendency. By partialling out the effects of social class, Miller demonstrated that the original correlations between these and four other factors and the achievement scores reduced by only .05. Incidentally, the achievement scores correlated .29 with social class.

The study by Miller showed that although there is a weak association between social class and educational attainment, other factors are more related to educational achievement. Two of these factors appear to be related to whether the child has some degree of autonomy. Perhaps the child who is an achiever at school is allowed to do things more on his own at home. It is difficult determining cause and effect here as parents of less intelligent children might be cautious about letting them do things too much themselves. Again, if a child wants to have a job requiring intellectual work, this could be because attainment at school is good in these kinds of activities. Finally, a child who feels rejected might be experiencing this because he or she is not intellectually so responsive to others, and thereby discourages social reciprocity. Thus this study is not clearly establishing the factors which might underlie scholastic achievement; these and other factors could be the result of achievement at school and/or the intellectual level of the child. This is not to say that the parents themselves have a part to play in exerting some influence on these factors.

One would think that if a child had parents who read magazines, newspapers and books frequently, the child would be more motivated to learn to read. Thus the parents would provide a model for the child to imitate. Furthermore, such parents might be more likely to read stories to the children and encourage them to delve into the imaginary worlds which unfold when reading a story book.

Clark (1970) isolated 19 severely backward readers from a group of about 1500 children aged 7 years in a Scottish county. She found by interviewing the parents, that although they were favourably disposed to education, very few of them actually read to their children. If there was any reading done this only involved the school reading primer. In a later contrasting study (1976) Clark examined 32 children who were reading well when they started school at 5 years of age. She noted that their social class, as defined by the father's occupation, was unimportant. Instead, "these homes were providing rich and exciting experiences within which books were indeed an integral part". However there is a connection between social class and parental reading in the general population in that in a survey in the UK asking people if they had read a book at least once in the last 4 weeks, 68% of professional people said "yes", compared with only 42% and 40% from the skilled and unskilled manual classes, respectively (Speddy, 1982).

Harding (1983), as part of her study on average and retarded readers matched on intelligence, sex and social class, found that both mothers and fathers of average readers read books, magazines and newspapers significantly more often than those of the retarded readers. Thus an environment in which parents are seen to be reading and obviously valuing the activity must be influential for the child. One alternative explanation could be that parents of retarded readers due to genetic reasons are also poor readers, so the lack of reading on the part of parents and the relationship of this to backward reading in children may be an effect of genetically transmitted reading retardation.

A study by Hansen (1973) has also shown that the parental environment is important for determining the extent to which children are positive about reading. Fourth grade children were tested on their degree of positive attitude toward reading. Then their mothers were given a questionnaire and the three most important items on the questionnaire, in terms of their correlation with the total score on the questionnaire were as follows: first, parental encouragement of homework in the early years; second, regular and large amounts of reading to the child from early on; third, the ability of the parent to name one or several books a child had read in the past month. Hansen concluded that such factors as socio-economic status, intelligence and whether the parent provided a model for reading behaviour were not so important as those factors listed previously. Instead the parent had to interact with the child and show an interest in his progress in reading.

There is evidence that the level of schooling of parents can determine the level of interaction with the children. Laosa (1982) has shown that in Chicano (Spanish-speaking) and white non-Hispanic families living in the USA there is a correlation of .33 between the frequency with which the mother reads to the child and the level of schooling of the mother. Furthermore, Laosa found a correlation in Chicanos of .28 between the percentage of children who learned to read before starting school and the schooling level of the mother. Thus, about 13% could read before school who were born of mothers who had undergone 6 years of schooling whereas 40% could read who were born of mothers who had experienced 11 to 14 years of schooling. The preschool literacy of the children did not correlate significantly with the schooling nor the occupation of the father. The picture is made more complex by the fact that Laosa found that in homes where the parents were better educated, parent-child interactions were in English, whereas in those of the lesser educated, Spanish was used more. It was concluded that the effect of schooling was to encourage particular types of communication between mother and child. Perhaps Chicano children who are poor academically at school, are at that level because of the contrast between their school and home environments.

Another major influence in the home, apart from that of parents, might be that of the television. Williams, Haertel, Haertel and Walberg (1982) examined 23 studies within different nations involving 277 correlations between measures of achievement at school and different estimates of viewing time. This produced a very low median correlation of -.06 overall, indicating that a longer amount of time watching television was related to poorer scholastic performance. Exactly the same correlation was obtained on 66 correlations between reading attainment and estimates of viewing time. Thus television has a slightly detrimental effect, but it is debatable whether this is because lengthy viewers have less time to read or because as they are slightly poorer readers, they prefer to watch television. What is surprising is how poor the relationship is between television watching time and reading performance.

2. THE INFLUENCE OF LANGUAGE

It is difficult working out precisely what aspects of lower socio-economic status contribute to difficulties in learning to read. One aspect of socio-economic status is the accompanying language usage which may contribute to the differences in reading performance. This difference in language could produce reading problems in several different ways.

One way, which as far as I know has not been considered so far, is that language differences are contributing an artifactual difference. Thus, when undergoing reading tests, the non-standard pronunciation of words and phraseology of working-class children is marked as incorrect. But in practice, they are able to extract the meaning from the text at a level commensurate with their standard-English speaking peer group.

A way to test this would be to see whether the gap in reading between the classes narrows when a form of comprehension recognition test is applied to a previously read passage compared with the more conventional reading performance test. This comprehension test might attempt to eliminate any class bias. Even if this aspect is non-artifactual, the experience of the child of being perceived by the teacher as being "incorrect" could no doubt lead to retardation in reading progress. Another possibility is that any form of language other than standard English is deficient and this in turn might lead to deficiencies in reading as reading itself is a language-based activity.

One problem for the writer of the reading primer is that the majority of children learning to read will not be speakers of standard English (or "received pronunciation"). Not only does working-class language differ from standard English, but it also varies across the regions of the United Kingdom. There are also other languages used in the United Kingdom other than English: Irish, Scots Gaelic, Welsh and at one time, Cornish. Many years ago British children were punished if they used any other language than English. For example, during British rule in Ireland, a tally-stick was notched each time Irish was spoken by a child. In Wales and Scotland a special stick was used to hit children if they ever spoke in their native tongue. However, a much more tolerant attitude now prevails towards the use of a child's language that would be used at home. In addition to the indigenous languages, there are of course the languages of successive generations of immigrants from Europe, the West Indies, Africa, India and Pakistan and so on.

Most research that has been carried out in this area has tended to concentrate on the language of black children living in the USA. Research indicates that these children can understand standard English and can translate it into their own vernacular. This is not surprising considering how much standard English must be heard on television and radio, as well as at school. Edwards (1979), reviewing the meagre evidence available on the effects of working-class or different ethnic languages on reading progress, concludes that the complex sound-spelling relationships which have to be learned when reading are probably no more difficult for Afro-American speakers than for ordinary white speakers. It has been suggested that initial reading primers might be written in black English vernacular. However this has been criticized; for instance, there is the problem that there are many different varieties of language. In addition, parents generally seem to be against the idea either because they feel that it would retard the social enhancement of their children or because they view their own language usage as inferior to standard English.

Edwards suggests that the prevalent climate of

tolerance toward varieties of language usage should continue. Thus children should be allowed to read a text using their own style of language. For example, a black American child might read <u>I asked Alvin if he knows how to play basketball</u> as follows "I acks Alvin do he know how to play basketball". Perhaps one component of the poorer reading of working-class children and children from other ethnic groups is that when undergoing reading tests, their non-standard pronunciation of words and phraseology is marked as incorrect. But in practice they are able to extract the meaning from the text at a level commensurate with their age.

The view was expressed earlier that working-class language within the various non-standard versions of English is somehow deficient in relation to standard English. This view has emerged partly due to the work of Bernstein (1958, 1961, 1971), although Bernstein himself would now subscribe to this "language deficit" viewpoint. Bernstein suggested two contrasting forms of language which he called the <u>restricted code</u> and the <u>elaborated code</u>. The restricted code is used by both middle- and working-class children during the course of ordinary conversation. It is essentially a simple language with a simple grammar. It is vague in dealing with abstract concepts and it is also accompanied by much arm waving. The elaborated code is only used by the middle-classes and is more precise and complicated.

Bernstein (1958) suggested that the formal setting of school is an environment where it is essential to use the elaborated code. The working-class child has a problem in dealing with the elaborated code as his background has equipped him to use only the more impoverished restricted code. Bernstein's notions have been substantiated to an extent by himself and others. For instance, Cook-Gumperz (1973) interviewed middle-class and working-class mothers and found these hypothesized distinctions, although there was much variation within each class. On the other hand, there are others, especially outside Britain, who have been unable to substantiate Bernstein. Davis (1977), for instance, was unable to do so in Australia.

Bernstein's ideas have had a considerable influence on subsequent research. As has been mentioned, there has been a focus on the issue of whether working-class language and ethnic languages are actually inferior to standard English or simply different. To summarize the argument against the language deficit notion: Labov (1969) has contended that the environment of the black American child is verbally very well-developed. This is based on research in natural settings. He suggests that the use of the restricted code is more desirable as it is more economical and simpler to understand. Middle-class speech, by contrast, is full of pauses and tends to have too many qualifications which obfuscate the intended meaning.

One aspect of the argument which is at least more objective is that black English vernacular appears to be just as rule-bound as standard English. For instance, Marwit, Marwit and Boswell (1972) gave black and white children a sentence completion task such as "This is a cup that belongs to the lun. Whose cup is it? It is the ___ ." The children consistently used the form of construction relevant to their background. Thus in the example, the black children said "It is the lun'". If black children have learned consistent grammatical rules, it could hardly be argued that the language they used was defective.

In the view of Edwards (1979) the difference-deficit controversy is now subsiding. There is growing agreement that the speech of the disadvantaged is a valid, rule-bound variety of speech. This agreement is not just among psychologists and linguists, but is spreading to speech clinicians as well. It might be tentatively suggested that although children of lower socio-economic status have a poorer standard of reading, the fact that their speech is generally different does not seem to be contributing to their reading problems.

3. IMPLICATIONS FOR HELPING POOR READERS

We have seen how important it is to have parents taking an interest in the reading of the child. Although there is a strong tendency for middle-class parents to take rather more of an interest in their children's academic performance than working-class parents, there are many working-class parents who also take a keen interest in this as well. It follows that any program of remediation which helps to foster an interest in parents in their children's performance should be a powerful incentive for their improvement in reading. One way of doing this is to

give parents a role in the remediation process.
Some parents of remedial readers may not be able to
read well themselves, but it is necessary that there
should be at least one parent who has an acceptable
level of reading ability.

A recent study of 16 schools in the North of
England by Hannon and Cuckle (1984) suggests that
most schools at present do not involve parents with
reading. They interviewed headmasters, teachers and
children and found that although there was an
acknowledgement by all the teachers of the
importance of parental involvement, only three out
of 20 guided all their parents about reading
instruction. A further four guided only parents of
problem readers. They also found that school books
were rarely used for home reading. Sixty children
were interviewed, but only two were taking a book
home on the date of interview.

Tizard, Schofield and Hewison (1982) studied
children from six schools in a working-class
multi-racial district of London. For a two-year
period children of 6 to 7 years of age in two
classes of two of the schools were given reading
homework set by the class teacher which had to be
heard by their parents. Comparison groups comprised
children from other classes within the same school
or other schools. One comparison group was given
extra teacher help instead of parental help and the
other group was given no extra help.

All parents agreed to the researcher visiting
them on two or three occasions to listen to the
child reading to the parents. Then the child read
to the researcher and the parents were advised on
certain points. There were a small number of
parents who appeared to be using poor strategies of
instruction to their children, and these had to be
altered. The parental response was enthusiastic and
with only two or three exceptions they cooperated
over the two years. The reading homework was
organized by the head and class teachers and the
researcher. The parents had to maintain a special
reading card. All children had homework at least
two times a week and usually three times a week. In
one school class this consisted of further reading
from the current class reader.

The result of the study was that there was a
significant improvement in the children experiencing
extra tuition by their parents, compared with their
control groups. On average, the home tutored
children had a standardized reading score (NFER) of

104 and the controls had a score of 95 which is a difference of 9 points. However, the children receiving extra tuition at school, experienced no similar improvement. The improvement in performance was brought about without giving the parents any special training in tutoring, except for brief demonstrations during the home monitoring periods.

A similar study by Coe (1971) in the USA on a much smaller scale on 18 grade 2 children, in which they were given help for 30 minutes each day for 5 months, also produced significant gains. By contrast, Snyder and Warden (1969) are critical of the idea of parental involvement and suggest that the effects could be harmful. They also suggest that parental tutoring is much more tolerated by girls than by boys and by younger rather than older children.

While the age of the child may be important in determining the success of parental intervention, the Tizard et al. study provides strong evidence in favour of encouraging parental support. But it is something that needs to be handled sensitively by teachers, as parents of remedial readers may be initially diffident about having contact with them. However, it is encouraging that Tizard et al. report a good deal of enthusiasm for the task by the parents once the programme was under way. There are several books available for parents who might wish to give their children reading tuition, such as Love (1970) and Stevenson (1974).

CHAPTER SUMMARY

There is a much higher incidence of reading problems within children of parents of lower socio-economic status. Two major aspects of differences between social classes are within the areas of parental attitudes and language usage.

Parental attitudes do seem to have an important role to play in reading development. In a group of severely backward readers hardly any of the parents read to their children; by contrast, in a group of advanced young readers the parents were providing a rich environment which included the frequent use of books (Clark, 1970, 1976). In the few studies within this area, parental encouragement appears to be of paramount importance and the socio-economic status of the parents appears to be less important. Another apparent environmental influence, that of the television, appears to have little effect on reading development.

An obvious difference between the social classes is in the use of language. It was suggested that working-class children could be scored as poorer at reading simply because their responses to reading a text were often marked as "incorrect" as they had used non-standard pronunciations or modes of expression. In fact, their reading performance and comprehension could be just as good.

Although there is not a good deal of data available on the influence of language on reading, there is a consensus view emerging that non-standard forms of English usage are not deficient forms of language. Therefore the use of these non-standard forms of English are not per se contributing to reading problems. Two of the arguments for this view are that these other forms of language are consistent in their rule structure and that the standard English speakers express themselves in too uneconomical a form, so received pronunciation is not necessarily superior.

In conclusion, it seems that the interest that the parents demonstrate in their children is the most important environmental influence on reading. One way to foster this interest is to involve the parents in supervising the reading homework of their children. Current research suggests that this is a very effective aspect of reading improvement. However in the United Kingdom generally (excluding N. Ireland which is different), primary school children are not given reading homework to do. It would be a good idea if reading homework was introduced.

Chapter Seven

THE THEORY AND PRACTICE OF LEARNING TO READ

        In this final chapter we are going to examine
briefly some theoretical perspectives about the
process of learning to read and then we will
summarize some changes in teaching and remedial
practice which should bring about gains in reading
performance.

1. THEORETICAL PERSPECTIVES OF READING

In this section we will confine ourselves to
explanations of why some children, despite average
intelligence, have difficulty with learning to read.
For any academic discipline to make adequate
progress, those working in it must try to develop a
theoretical structure. Principles or hypotheses
must be established which are amenable to scientific
investigation and which hopefully provide guidelines
for the practitioner to work along. Unfortunately
it seems to me that a good deal of research in
reading is investigating isolated hypotheses without
much theoretical work being carried out of a more
integrative nature.
        As we shall see, some theories of reading are
more like conceptual frameworks or metaphysical
theories, which although not testable, help to set
experimental findings within a particular
perspective. They may also have the role of being a
catalyst for further research. In order to be
scientific, it is important that theories should be
capable of being potentially falsifiable. In other
words, theories (or hypotheses) should make
predictions which experimenters can test.
Scientific theories should also be causal as
discussed before, near the beginning of Chapter 4.
We will now examine various perspectives in theories

of learning to read, which will entail a certain degree of overlap in the contents of each section.

The maturational lag perspective

This approach has already been discussed at length elsewhere. Let us review the main points that have been made about this approach so far. It proposes that poor readers are lagging behind in the development of certain skills and that these skills have to be developed to a certain level before reading can commence properly. Satz and his co-workers, who have been the main proponents, make specific proposals concerning which skills should develop and the periods when these skills are demonstrating their fastest progress. These specific proposals have not been well supported, but there is experimental evidence that retarded readers matched with normal readers of the same age and nonverbal intelligence are less well developed in certain other cognitive skills and in bone growth. No doubt further research will elucidate other areas of retardation in development.

In assessing a theory it is important to consider its alternatives. In this case, maturational lag theory proposes that retarded readers are lagging behind in the development of prerequisite skills for reading. One commonly proposed alternative is that retarded readers have a deficit in certain cognitive processes. This alternative supposes that these children actually sustain permanent damage in critical areas of the brain. Indeed in a previous chapter we demonstrated how certain areas of the brain were implicated in the reading process. This brain damage slows down or eliminates processing within specific areas. Consequently, in order to get reading under way other less specialized areas of the brains of these retarded readers would be brought into use. But as these areas are inferior the children progress at a much slower rate. This brain damage alternative seems to make predictions which are actually very close to a maturational lag explanation – almost to the point where the two explanations are identical. Both suggest retarded development in certain processes. But is not retardation in the development of a process similar to or the same as "damage" to the area within which that process is supposed to take place? If one could pinpoint areas of neurological damage within retarded readers, this

would be evidence in favour of not only a deficit,
for a maturational lag theory could handle this as
well. Similarly, if there were no areas of
neurological damage, at first glance, this supports
a maturational lag theory; but it could be argued
that there might still be damage, but it is not as
yet detectable by present-day instrumentation. The
two theories do not seem to be clearly
distinguishable.

Another alternative to a maturational lag
theory is that retarded readers are normal in all
respects except that their reading is poor. In
other words, they are deficient only in those
processes necessary to reading. Consequently all
those processes which are enhanced in normal
children as a result of being able to read are, by
contrast, less well developed in poor readers. This
theory, if it may be so graced by this rubric, may
be considered from a statistical viewpoint. All
things in nature have variation. There is variation
in the width of leaves falling from the same tree,
adults vary in weight, and so on. The same applies
to a skill such as art-work: some people are good
artists and others have very little skill in this
direction. By the same token, in reading some
children are slower to learn to read than others.

Insofar as a maturational lag explanation has
made a contribution, one aspect of this particular
alternative explanation has been disproved by the
experimental evidence. If poor readers are simply
poor within those processes necessary to reading,
this implies that those processes normally enhanced
by the reading process in normal readers will be
retarded in poor readers. For instance, it might be
that normal readers become more aware of the actual
sounds in words as a result of learning to read.
However, poor readers are deficient in areas in
which one would not expect a deficiency due to lack
of experience in reading. For instance, poor
readers have a poor short-term memory. However,
even this particular deficit might be due to
retarded phonemic processing which in turn is due to
lack of experience in reading. This is because
there is a link between slow output and poor
performance on the digit span (Nicholson, 1981).
Thus children impaired phonemically and who can not
articulate quickly do worse on the digit span even
though their actual retentive capabilities might be
normal. It should be noted that this "simply poor
readers" alternative theory is also very similar to

a maturational lag theory. The only difference is that other processes are capable of lagging under the terms of the maturational lag theory. Thus the alternative examined here is actually a form of the maturational lag hypothesis.

A final alternative to a maturational lag explanation is one couched in terms of the kind of strategies that the child uses. The child in order to learn to read needs to be aware of certain aspects of the reading process. For example, he needs to know that one symbol usually represents one sound or that one collection of symbols represents one word. It might be that this metacognitive awareness is not apparent merely because the child has not been taught these aspects of reading. Thus reading retardation may be due to the operation of a poor strategy on the part of the child.

How is this an alternative to the theory of a maturational lag? Maturational lag theory is usually conceptualized as "... the developmental pattern of brain maturation from birth to maturity" (Satz and Sparrow, 1970). An explanation in terms of psychological strategies is not strongly related to explanations in terms of physiological development. To use the analogy of a computer, Physiology is concerned with the structure of the wiring in the computer, whereas Psychology is more concerned with the programs that run within the computer.

But again, testing this strategy theory alternative against the maturational lag hypothesis is difficult. Suppose children were given training in order to change their strategies and approaches to reading and there was a subsequent improvement in their reading. This could be taken as support for both alternatives. Changing the child's strategy had improved his reading, supporting a strategies explanation; but it may also have accelerated development in those cognitive areas specialized in these particular skills, also supporting a maturational lag explanation. However, if this improvement was sufficiently fast, this would add considerable weight to a strategies explanation. Beech and Harding (1984) have suggested the use of the term "developmental lag" to straddle across the lags in development produced by underlying physiological structures and/or the effects of environmental factors.

It can be seen that there are no serious alternatives to a maturational lag explanation of reading. In a sense it could be argued that the theory is unscientific in that it is impossible to disprove. In its starkest form it could be stated that children who are slow at learning to read are this way because they are slow in learning to read. Seen in the light of a tautologous hypothesis, we might regard the maturational lag hypothesis more as a conceptual framework to examine reading performance rather than a scientific hypothesis. Thus it provokes questions concerning which underlying skills fail to develop which in turn affect reading, whether there is a strictly biological lag or whether training can expedite development, and so on.

The prerequisite skills perspective

This might be better described as the prerequisite skills assumption. It underlies innumerable studies in reading. It assumes that poor readers are backward along the dimension(s) measured by the experimenter relative to a control group of average readers who are matched in chronological age and intelligence. It could be the case (but it does not necessarily follow) that these dimensions are part or wholly the prerequisite skills the child needs in order to achieve an acceptable standard of reading. In order to establish some kind of causal connection here, an experimental design should be executed in which the poor readers are trained along these dimensions and consequently achieve an improvement in their standard of reading relative to a control group of poor readers who have been given training along different dimensions. However, very often experimental studies are content to fall far short of this design by merely indicating yet another area of deficit in the retarded reader. A group of retarded readers is compared with a control group and the retarded readers are found to be worse than the controls. It is concluded that the dimension under study indicates a deficit within the retarded reader.

In terms of the experimental evidence, the prerequisite skills assumption is not entirely plausible. It has problems in accounting for those very young children who are precocious readers. For example, Soderbergh (1976) reports on ten children in Stockholm between two and five years of age, of whom five were severely impaired in hearing and two were completely deaf who had learned to read! If it can be demonstrated that children are deficient in these hypothesized dimensions and yet are still able to learn to read, this casts serious doubt on the prerequisite skills assumption. However the assumption is not falsifiable, because it can always be claimed that there are certain other, as yet undiscovered prerequisite skills, which underlie reading and on which these younger children were normal.

Although the Soderbergh study suggests that young children without certain cognitive skills are nevertheless able to read, there is evidence that certain levels of cognitive skills may underlie reading development. We have already examined the work of Bradley and Bryant (1983) demonstrating that training in phonemic awareness skills in those children severely deficient in such skills, enhances their subsequent reading performance. This is comparing against a group of children with a similar level of deficiency, but trained on an irrelevant semantic categorization task. Overall it seems that a deficiency in phonemic awareness is sometimes, but not always, associated with reading impairment. If there is a causal connection, other conditions need to be present in order to produce this causal connection. At the present time our picture is incomplete as we do not yet know the nature of these other conditions.

Single vs multiple factor theories of reading

Carr (1981) has noted that most theories of reading have advocated a single factor which lies behind poor reading. He suggests that it would be more realistic to develop theories which account for more than one factor. Let us examine his thesis in detail.

Most of the single factor theories he described have already been dealt with: visual discrimination, phonological and **semantic recoding**, short-term memory and utilization of linguistic knowledge and context. But his section on short-term memory needs further brief coverage. One problem with explaining poor reading in terms of a poor short-term memory is that short-term memory subserves a large part of cognitive processing so that it can account for a wide variety of processes. One form of the short-term memory deficit hypothesis proposes an inability to keep several chunks of information maintained in short-term memory.

Another form suggests problems with the order in which items occurred rather than the quantity of information. Yet another form suggests that the poor reader is inefficient in handling information passing to and from short-term memory (Perfetti and Lesgold, 1978). This theory proposes the development of a cumulative lag (or "hysteresis") in information entering short-term memory which in turn interferes with comprehension.

Carr modified this last form of the memory deficit hypothesis as follows. Suppose that a limited resource system was required for recoding the visual information from the words being read and also to put into storage the activated codes. If there is a problem in that part of the system dealing with visual information, less resources would be available on the storage side (see also Baddeley, 1979). This would lead to an increase in the information lost within short-term memory which in turn would affect overall comprehension. These theoretical formulations highlight the problems concerned with making interpretations about the undoubted poorer short-term memory of poor readers, a major problem being that a poor short-term memory can cause impairments in a variety of areas.

Turning to the use of multi-factor theories of reading, Carr comments on the need to assess the relative effect of different component skills on individual differences in reading performance. His own theorizing tends to concentrate on the older reader by examining the relationship between certain cognitive abilities and particular component tasks. For example, examining the work of Singer and Crouse (1981), Carr noted that they found that knowledge of **vocabulary** and cloze performance were direct predictors of comprehension of previously read passages. The cloze technique evaluates the reader's ability to predict what words come next in a text which abruptly stops. They found that the cloze technique in turn was directly predicted by vocabulary knowledge and performance on Raven's Progessive Matrices, which is a task measuring the extent of predictive reasoning. Thus readers who have a larger set of words capable of being used and who are also good at predictive reasoning, also do well on the cloze task. Continuing in this manner Carr derived a hierarchical model of the relationship among the various cognitive skills measured by Singer and Crouse.

Carr's approach has much to recommend it as

there is a need for more comprehensive models of reading. Of course, it might be criticised for including very little relevant to the development of reading; and tangentially, not much relates to our main focus concerning why it is that some children have difficulty in learning to read. To some extent working backwards from skilled readers, discovering more about how they process words and then relating this to beginning readers could be worthwhile.

A final criticism about the kind of model building advocated by Carr is that it is concerned more with specifying the interrelationships between different experimental tests relating to reading (e.g. Raven's matrices, etc.) than with the actual hypothesized processes underlying these tests. Admittedly when defining a process it is important to have that test "operationally defined", that is, to specify how that process is manifested experimentally. A more preferable model, within the area in which Carr is concerned, might specify the interrelationships between speed of access into the internal dictionary, the higher-order ability of the child to make inferences about how the text is likely to proceed and the lower-order capabilities of making letter-to-sound conversions.

Let us discuss a little further the reading process in the adult and then relate this to the child. When I match my own phenomenal experience of reading with what we know from research on alexia, there is a paradox. When reading I am personally aware of a mechanical process translating the print and a concurrent higher-order semantic process, often utilizing imagery. The reasons will be elaborated later. And yet, if there is any distinction between reading processes, according to the brain-damage work there seems to be a functional system which contains a sight-vocabulary of words and a processor which is capable of translating letter-by-letter. This is because there are patients who can recognize whole words, presumably within their sight-vocabulary, but not non-words. Similarly, there are other patients who take an increasing amount of time to read words as a function of letter length. These patients appear to have an impaired sight-vocabulary and instead read letter-by-letter. All alexic patients appear to have normal comprehension, so the higher-order processes do not seem to be impaired.

The reason for making a distinction between the mechanical process of reading print and higher-order processes is that I sometimes experience myself wandering away in thought from the theme of what is being read and yet the mechanical process of reading (in terms of eye-scanning, etc.) appears to continue, if only momentarily. Similarly, I can read aloud to a child a bedtime story and be thinking of something else at the same time; in other words, I am not processing the story I am reading to a higher level. Thus reading for the adult might be regarded as a limited resource system over which there is some limited degree of conscious control. Another example of this control is that we can change from high speed scanning of text to slower word-by-word reading. Again, we can scan through text from many different perspectives, scanning at one time for grammar, at another for punctuation, spelling and so on.

In parenthesis, the paradox between the alexia work and the phenomenal experience of reading could be resolved by assuming that the dichotomy unearthed by the alexia work may by concerned with processes outside our consciousness. When we try to tap these particular processes experimentally we might adjust the reader's (unconscious?) strategies to operate in a manner different from normal reading, especially within experiments on reaction times to one- or two-word stimuli.

The child has to develop a certain level of competence at the mechanical skill of reading. By contrast, the mental equipment capable of higher-order processing should already be available, because the normal child enjoys conversation, listening to stories and so on. However, the resources required in these early stages are mainly required at the lower mechanical level, such as translating letters to sounds. Furthermore the information that becomes available as a result of this lower-order process may be too patchy for the child to make much sense of what is being read. The evidence suggests that the poor reader is poor at these mechanical skills and furthermore is not well equipped to hold these fragments of information in memory while some meaning is generated. A resources model beginning on this basis, outlining the components of this dynamic process, might serve as a useful basis for understanding the problems children have learning to read; and hopefully, it might suggest those processes on which the teacher should concentrate. Anderson (1980), LaBerge and Samuels (1974) and Perfetti and Lesgold (1978) and indeed

Carr, have all made some progress in this direction.

2. TEACHING CHILDREN TO LEARN TO READ

It would be very nice to be able to follow on from a discussion of theories of reading by outlining the implications of these theories for teachers. However this is not to be, at least not directly. Instead, let me summarize the most important points made in previous chapters by making concrete suggestions concerning what teachers might try out in their classroom.

What the teacher might do

Let us start with children who at the age of 4 and 5 years are starting school for the first time. Soon after starting school a simple test of their phonemic awareness could be given. For instance, they might be given pictures of objects (say three at a time) and asked to put together the two pictures that end with the same sounds (e.g. "house" and "mouse"). Several sets of pictures would be given and an overall score produced. Children who have difficulty with this task, as shown by a low score, thereafter would be given a systematic training programme over the following months developing their phonemic awareness. All children could be taught a gradually expanding set of letters using the tracing technique, as well as being started on a sight-vocabulary of words.

Even at this stage it would help if the teacher contacted parents and ensured that each child was being read a bedtime story at least two or three times each week. The main purpose of this would be to start an involvement of the parents with their children in terms of reading and for the children to associate interesting stories with the reading process. This activity should be monitored and encouraged for at least the next three years. Parental involvement might be approached at a more formal level by setting parents a programme of reading material.

In Britain it is the practice in many schools not to let a proportion of children come into school until they are 5 years of age, starting in the spring term. The problem with this is that it exaggerates age differences between the children by giving these late entrants a substantial

120

disadvantage relative to the rest of the class. It would probably be better for these younger children to start in September of the previous year when they are still 4 years of age. Northern Ireland, for example, has children starting school at this age and this seems quite workable. Thus all the children in a first class would experience the same amount of schooling, starting from September.

At the end of their first year, a reading test needs to be given. Appendix 1 gives the most recent standardized ages for the Schonell reading test. Parents are strongly advised not to apply this test to their children, if they are in a position to do so. This could distort the measured reading age of their child when professionals come to use the test later. On the basis of this reading test and depending on what resources are available, a decision might be made as to which children could benefit from remedial help in the following year. It may well be that such remedial help in the second year will save remedial resources in later years.

During the second year and after that, teachers will be aiming to give children constant practice at their skills at decoding letters to sounds as well as vice-versa in terms of their writing. Gradually comprehension processes will be emphasized more and more. It has been noted previously that as children get older they are increasingly given a lot of work purportedly developing their comprehension skills but in reality this does not develop their reading capabilities. This means that tests of comprehension need to test a genuine understanding of the materials, rather than a superficial reproduction of the original text. As reading progresses, teachers might switch to using the Neale Analysis of Reading instead of the Schonell. This will help identify children who may have good reading skills but who are poor at comprehension. These were called "poor integrators" in Chapter 3. Teachers should also encourage parents to transfer from reading to their children to listening to their children reading on a regular basis. It is important that this reading should be interactive, in other words, the pictures should be examined and the story talked about. Research has shown that such involvement of parents has a powerful effect on reading progress.

Some research on language and intelligence enhancement suggests that if the father is involved as well in the programme, this brings about

121

additional benefits. Some schools in Londonderry are involved in a research programme in which the parents visit the school for one hour a week and are given guidance by teachers and volunteers. This programme, involving Bill Donaghy and others, is not focussed directly on reading but on general intellectual development (see Donaghy, 1976, 1979).

Mention has been made of the importance of promoting an interest in reading. A regular change of activity throughout the day can be helpful. Games involving word-building could be employed from time to time, such as "Hangman" or "Scrabble". Team games could be arranged in which a crossword is set and teams of three or four race to complete the crossword on the board. Progress charts help sustain an interest for individual children. The use of these coupled with stars and tokens for individual pieces of work all help to encourage and motivate the child. But it would be detrimental to punish the child by moving a child's progress downwards on the chart!

Research has shown that teachers are often unaware of the particular interests of their children. Of course, these interests can be quite changeable. However efforts should be made to provide reading materials which match these topic interests. Encouraging children to visit their local libraries could be very useful. This could be arranged by the whole class visiting the library by arrangement and by encouraging parents to sustain this interest. If the teacher has several copies of the same story book, she could read aloud to a group of children and stop at an exciting part and invite all of them to continue to read silently the rest of the story. A quiet environment would be important for such an exercise.

A development on the horizon which could be exceedingly useful is that of the microcomputer for the teaching of reading. This would enable children to progress at their own pace. The technology is now available for programs to generate speech in the form of what sounds like a robot's voice. Each extra computer in the classroom could almost be the equivalent to having an extra teacher in the classroom. Children do take to machines extraordinarily well; they love watching colourful pictures and making responses to them. In contrast to most things, a computer seems to be capable of sustaining their attention for long periods of time. Given this, it should be an ideal medium for aiding the teacher in the classroom. Good bibliographical sources to research in this area are Mason and Blanchard (1979) and Wilkinson (1983).

What society might do

There are several steps which our society could take in dealing with the reading problem. One of these is perhaps more of a pipe dream than a reality. A reform of our present spelling system in order to make spelling more regular would be very useful for the beginning reader. There can be no question that children learning a regularly spelled system would learn to read and spell much faster. For instance, children learning the previously described ita system, which is in the main regularly spelled, read in that system considerably faster than children learning to read in present-day spelling. Unfortunately, these children then have to transfer to normal spelling which takes them so long that they eventually lose the advantage that they had gained; thus after three years they are at the same level as children who started off learning words spelled normally. Nevertheless, the ita experiment has demonstrated that our present spelling system is an impediment to learning to read. Downing (1967) showed in an experiment that after about two years, half the children reading in ita finished the reading scheme, but only one-quarter of the control sample reading normal spelling had reached this point.

Beech (1980, 1983) has reviewed the arguments for spelling reform and has shown that in practice a mild reform can be adjusted to fairly easily by adults. Many other countries have made spelling reforms, some quite recently, but English is perhaps the one language which remains unchanged and which is the most irregular, in terms of a system which has a rough correspondence between letters and sounds. Perhaps even worse are systems having a different symbol representing each word, such as in part of Japanese writing.

Some of the counter-arguments for reform may be briefly summarised as follows. First, and most importantly, it would be very expensive to change the present stock of books to the new spelling. Second, many adults could find it difficult to cope with a new spelling system. Third, spelling sometimes helps to differentiate the meaning of the words sounding the same (e.g. "to", "too", and "two"). Fourth, our present spelling also shows how the word derives from another language. Finally, it shows similarities between words which may have been lost as pronunciations have evolved (e.g. "sign", "signal").

A more practical direction authorities might take is concerned with the career structure of the remedial reading teacher. Her position is not regarded as a high one within the school hierarchy. Certainly, no teacher aspiring for promotion would jump at the opportunity to become a remedial teacher. She has to be good at social relationships as she needs the close cooperation of other teachers in the school. She may find occasionally that she is passed a child with behaviour problems rather than reading problems, to give the class teacher a respite. If any teacher is suddenly ill, she may find herself stepping into the breach to take over a class. Also she may find that the facilities available are poor; for instance, she may be given a make-shift room in a noisy environment or even be placed at the back of the class. Furthermore, there may not be a great deal of variety of reading matter available to her.

This low-level role needs to be reversed. The remedial teacher should be a specialist on the subject of reading to whom other class teachers come for help and advice. She should play a major part, perhaps in consultation with the class teacher, in deciding who needs to be taken out and given further help and who no longer needs remedial help. She might initiate and supervise programmes of voluntary help. Remedial teaching ought to have a career structure which will attract more of the best people in the teaching profession. Universities ought to offer part-time courses on remediation leading to a special diploma or Masters degree.

One other direction that our society could take in coping with the reading problem may already have taken place. That is, our society is becoming more tolerant towards those who have difficulty in reading. Gradually we have become aware that there are adults with such difficulties. The adult literacy scheme has been very successful in educating the public about this. Traffic signs etc. have changed from written text to symbols; although the motivation to do this was perhaps more to accommodate foreign language speakers. But in more general terms, there is a greater tolerance, for instance, within our educational system towards individuals unable to spell. There are sometimes rumblings from the occasional academic or employer complaining of deteriorating standards. But at least there has generally been a less hostile environment for the bright person who has problems with reading. Also, one or two show business personalities have revealed that they still have serious problems with reading which in turn has helped the prevailing mood of tolerance.

Looking to the future, technology may shift our attitudes even further in this direction. Machines which can read aloud books, originally designed for the blind, have been developed. Television has hastened our independence from reading by providing entertainment when a generation or two previously mainly books and newspapers were all that was available for entertainment - although as we have seen, television viewing does not adversely affect reading standards to any great extent. Furthermore, other technological developments, such as computers in the classroom, will help children to read. The recent development of teletext, for instance, may be a further stimulus to the child to translate the seemingly strange symbols that we call words and to discover what lies beyond.

REFERENCES

Aaron, P.G., Baxter, C. and Lucenti, J. (1980).
Developmental dyslexia and acquired dyslexia: two
sides of the same coin? Brain and Language, 11, 1
- 11.
Alexander, D. and Money, J. (1965). Reading
ability, object constancy and Turner's syndrome.
Perceptual and Motor Skills, 20, 981 - 4.
Allen, M. (1983). Models of hemispheric
specialization. Psychological Bulletin, 93, 73 -
104.
Anderson, J. R. (1980). Cognitive Psychology and
its implications. San Francisco: W. H. Freeman
and Co.
Anderson, R. C. and Kulhavy, R.W. (1972).
Imagery and prose learning. Journal of
Educational Psychology, 63, 242 - 243.
Askov, E. N. (1982). Role of the teacher in
fostering comprehension of expository text:
Comparison of theory and practices advocated in
teacher education textbooks. In W. Otto and S.
White (eds.), Reading expository material.
London: Academic Press.
Augur, J. (1982). Language structure and
multi-sensori techniques. Paper presented at the
Northern Ireland Speech and Language Forum
Conference. Belfast City Hospital, October, 1982.
Baddeley, A. D. (1979). Working memory and
reading. In P. A. Kolers, M. E. Wrolstad and
H. Bouma (eds.), Processing of visible language
1. New York: Plenum.
Baddeley, A. D., Ellis, N. C. and Miles, T. R.
(1982). Developmental and acquired dyslexia: a
comparison. Cognition, 11, 185 - 199.
Bamberger, R. (1976). Literature and development
in reading. In J. E. Merritt (ed.), New

126

horizons in reading. Newark, Del: International
Reading Association.
Barr, R. (1974 - 1975). The effect of instruction
on pupil reading strategies. Reading Research
Quarterly, 10, 555 - 82.
Barr, R. (1982). Readers knowledge and classroom
instruction. In W. Otto and S. White (eds.),
Reading expository material. London: Academic
Press.
Bartlett, F. C. (1932). Remembering. Cambridge:
Cambridge University Press.
Barton, A. H. (1963). Reading research and its
communication: the Columbia-Carnegie project. In
J. A. Figurel (ed.), Reading as an intellectual
activity. Newark, Del: International Reading
Association.
Beaumont, J. G. and Rugg, M. D. (1978).
Neuropsychological laterality of function and
dyslexia: a new hypothesis. Dyslexia Review, 1,
18 - 21.
Beech, J. R. (1980). Some proposed principles for
simplifying English orthography. Spelling
Progress Bulletin, 20, 7 - 13.
Beech, J. R. (1983). The effects of spelling
change on the adult reader. Spelling Progress
Bulletin, 13, 11 - 18.
Beech, J. R. and Harding, L. M. (1984).
Phonemic processing and the backward reader from a
developmental lag viewpoint. Reading Research
Quarterly, 19, 357 - 366.
Beery, J. (1967). Matching of auditory and visual
stimuli by average and retarded readers. Child
Development, 38, 827 - 833.
Bender, L. A. (1938). Visual Motor Gestalt Test
and its clinical use. (Research Monograph No. 3)
New York: American Orthopsychiatric Association.
Bender, L. A. (1956). Psychopathology of children
with organic brain disorders. Springfield, Ill:
Charles C. Thomas.
Benson, D. F. (1981). Alexia and the
neuroanatomical basis of reading. In F. J.
Pirozzolo and M. C. Wittrock (eds.),
Neuropsychological and cognitive processes in
reading. London: Academic Press.
Benton, A. L. (1962). Dyslexia in relation to
form perception and directional sense. In J.
Money (ed.), Reading disability: Progress and
research needs in dyslexia. Baltimore: Johns
Hopkins University Press.
Benton, A. L. (1978). Some conclusions about

dyslexia. In A. L. Benton and D. Pearl (eds.),
Dyslexia: An appraisal of current knowledge. New
York: Oxford University Press.

Benton, A. L. and Pearl, D. (eds.) (1978).
Dyslexia: An appraisal of current knowledge. New
York: Oxford University Press.

Bernstein, B. (1958). Some sociological
determinants of perception: An enquiry into
sub-cultural differences. British Journal of
Sociology, 9, 159 - 174.

Bernstein, B. (1961). Social class and linguistic
development: A theory of social learning. In A.
H. Halsey, J. Floud and C. A. Anderson (eds.),
Education, economy and society. New York: The
Free Press.

Bernstein, B. (1971). Class codes and control.
Vol. 1. London: Routledge and Kegan Paul.

Bieger, E. (1974). Effectiveness of visual
perceptual training on reading skills of
non-readers: An experimental study. Perceptual
and Motor Skills, 38 (3, Part 2), 1147 - 53.

Bieger, E. (1978). Effectiveness of visual
training of letters and words on reading skills of
non-readers. Journal of Educational Research, 71,
157 - 161.

Biemiller, A. (1970). The development of the use
of graphic and contextual information as children
learn to read. Reading Research Quarterly, 6, 75
- 96.

Birch, H. and Belmont, L. (1964). Auditory-visual
integration in normal and retarded readers.
American Journal of Orthopsychiatry, 34, 852 -
861.

Blank, M. (1968). Cognitive processes in auditory
discrimination in normal and retarded readers.
Child Development, 39, 1091 - 1101.

Blank, M. (1978). Review of "Toward an
understanding of dyslexia: Psychological factors
in specific reading disability". in A. L.
Benton and D. Pearl (eds.), Dyslexia: An
appraisal of current knowledge. New York: Oxford
University Press.

Blank, M., Berenzweig, S. S. and Bridger, W. H.
(1975). The effects of stimulus complexity and
sensory modality on reaction time in normal and
retarded readers. Child Development, 46, 133 -
140.

Boder, E. M. (1973). Developmental dyslexia: a
diagnostic approach based on three atypical
reading-spelling patterns. Developmental Medicine

and Child Neurology, 15, 663 - 87.

Bradley, L. and Bryant, P. E. (1978).
Difficulties in auditory organization as a
possible cause of reading backwardness. Nature,
271, 746 - 747.

Bradley, L. and Bryant, P. (1982). Reading skills
and categorizing sounds: a causal study involving
longitudinal prediction and intervention. Paper
presented at the British Psychological Society
Conference, University of London Institute of
Education, December.

Bradley, L. and Bryant P. E. (1983).
Categorizing sounds and learning to read - a
causal connection. Nature, 301, 419 - 421.

Bradshaw, J. L., Bradley, D., Gates, A. and
Patterson, K. (1977). Serial, parallel or
wholistic identification of single words in the
two visual fields? Perception and Psychophysics,
21, 431 - 38.

Bradshaw, J.L. and Nettleton, N. C. (1981). The
nature of hemispheric specialization in man. The
Behavioral and Brain Sciences, 4, 51 - 91.

Bryant, P.E. (1974). Perception and understanding
in young children. New York: Basic Books.

Bryden, M. P. (1972). Auditory-visual and
sequential-spatial matching in relation to reading
ability. Child Development, 43, 824 - 832.

Byrne, B. and Shea, P. (1979). Semantic and
phonetic memory codes in beginning readers.
Memory and Cognition, 7, 333 - 338.

Carmon, A. (1981). Temporal processing and the
left hemisphere. The Behavioral and Brain
Sciences, 4, 66 - 67.

Carr, T. H. (1981). Building theories of reading
ability: on the relation between individual
differences in cognitive skills and reading
comprehension. Cognition, 9, 73 - 114.

Chall, J. S. (1967). Learning to read: the great
debate. New York: McGraw-Hill.

Chansky, N. M. (1963). Age, IQ, and improvement
in reading. Journal of Educational Research, 56,
439.

Clark, M. M. (1970). Reading difficulties in
schools. Penguin Books: Harmondsworth.

Clark, M. M. (1976). Young fluent readers: what
can they teach us? London: Heinemann.

Coe, M. A. (1971). Parental involvement in
remedial reading instruction. Academic Therapy
Quarterly, 6 (4), 407 - 10.

Coltheart, M. (1980). Deep dyslexia: a right

hemisphere hypothesis. In M. Coltheart, K. Patterson and J. Marshall (eds.), Deep dyslexia. London: Routledge and Kegan Paul.

Cook-Gumperz, J. (1973). Social control and socialization: a study of class differences in the language of maternal control. London: Routledge and Kegan Paul.

Cromer, W. (1970). The difference model: a new explanation for some reading difficulties. Journal of Educational Psychology, 61, 471 - 483.

Crowder, R. G. (1982). The psychology of reading: an introduction. Oxford: Oxford University Press.

Curr, W. and Hallworth, H. J. (1965). An empirical study of the concept of retardation. Educational Review, 18, 5 - 15.

Davis, D. F. (1977). Language and social class: Conflict with established theory. Research in the Teaching of Reading. 11, 207 - 217.

De Hirsch, K., Jansky, J. and Langford, W. (1966). Predicting reading failure. New York: Harper and Row.

DeArmond, S. J., Fusco, M. M. and Dewey, M. M. (1976). Structure of the human brain: a photographic atlas. New York: Oxford University Press.

Denckla, M. B. and Rudel, R. G. (1976). Naming of object drawings by dyslexic and other learning disabled children. Brain and Language, 3, 1 - 15.

Deutsch, C. P. (1964). Auditory discrimination and learning: social factors. Merrill Palmer Quarterly, 10, 277 - 96.

Doehring, D. G. (1978). The tangled web of behavioral research on developmental dyslexia. In A. L. Benton and D. Pearl (eds.), Dyslexia: an appraisal of current knowledge. New York: Oxford University Press.

Donachy, W. (1976). Parent participation in pre-school education. British Journal of Educational Psychology, 46, 31 - 3.

Donaghy, W. (1979). Chapters 9 - 12. In M. M. Clark and W. M. Cheyne (eds.), Studies in pre-school education. London: Hodder and Stoughton.

Downing, J. A. (1967). Evaluating the ita. Cassell: London.

Drake, W. (1968). Clinical and pathological findings in a child with a developmental learning disability. Journal of Learning Disabilities, 1, 468 - 475.

130

Durkin, D. (1978-79). What classroom observations reveal about reading comprehension instruction. Reading Research Quarterly, 14, 481 - 533.

Edwards, J. R. (1979). Language and disadvantage. London: Edward Arnold.

Ellis, A. W. (1979). Developmental and acquired dyslexia: some observations on Jorm (1979). Cognition, 7, 413 - 420.

Fernald, G. M. and Keller, H. B. (1921). The effect of kinaesthetic factors in the development of word recognition in the case of the non-readers. Journal of Educational Research, 4, 355 - 77.

Fox, B. and Routh, D. K. (1980). Phonemic analysis and severe reading disability in children. Journal of Psycholinguistic Research, 9, 115 - 120.

Frostig, M., Maslow, P., LeFever, D. W. and Whittlesey, J. R. B. (1964). Marianne Frostig Development Test of Visual Perception. Perceptual and Motor Skills, 19, 463 - 499.

Funnell, E. (1983). Phonological processes in reading: new evidence from acquired dyslexia. British Journal of Psychology, 74, 159 - 180.

Galaburda, A. M. (1982). Neuroanatomical aspects of language and dyslexia. In Y. Zotterman (ed.), Dyslexia: neuronal, cognitive and linguistic aspects. Oxford: Pergamon.

Galaburda, A. M. and Kemper, T. (1979). Cytoarchitectonic abnormalities in developmental dyslexia: a case study. Annals of Neurology, 6, 94 - 100.

Gazzaniga, M. A. (1967). The split brain in man. Scientific American, 217, No. 2, 24 - 29.

Gibson, E. J. (1970). The ontogeny of reading. American Psychologist, 25, 136 - 143.

Golinkoff, R. M. (1975-76). A comparison of reading comprehension processes in good and poor comprehenders. Reading Research Quarterly, 11, 623 - 659.

Guthrie, J. T., Seifert, M. and Kline, L. W. (1978). Clues from research on programs for poor readers. In Samuels, S. J. (ed.), What research has to say about reading instruction. Newark, Del: International Reading Association.

Hannon, P. W. and Cuckle, P. (1984). Involving parents in the teaching of reading: a study of current school practice. Educational Research, 26, 7 -13.

Hansen, H. S. (1973). The home literacy

environment - a follow-up report. Elementary
English, 50, 97 - 98, 122.
Harding, L. M. (1983). The relationship between
reading ability and developmental levels in
primary school children. D. Phil. thesis
submitted to the New University of Ulster.
Harris, A. J. (1957). Lateral dominance,
directional confusion and reading disability.
Journal of Psychology, 44, 283 - 294.
Harris, A. J. (1977). The reading teacher as
diagnostician. In E. A. Earle (ed.), Classroom
practice in reading. Newark, Del: International
Reading Association.
Harris, A. J. and Sipay, E. R. (1980). How to
increase reading ability. New York: Longman.
Hicks, C. and Spurgeon, P. (1982). Two factor
analytic studies of dyslexic sub-types. British
Journal of Educational Psychology, 52, 289 - 300.
Hogaboam, T. and Perfetti, C. A. (1978). Reading
skill and the role of verbal experience in
decoding. Journal of Educational Psychology, 70,
717 - 729.
Holmes, J. M. (1973). Dyslexia: a
neurolinguistic study of traumatic and
developmental disorders of reading. Ph.D.
submitted to the University of Edinburgh.
Holmes, J. M. (1978). 'Regression' and reading
breakdown. In A. Caramazza and E. Zurif (eds.),
Language acquisition and language breakdown.
Baltimore: Johns Hopkins University Press.
Hulme, C. (1981). Reading retardation and
multi-sensory teaching. London: Routledge and
Kegan Paul.
Hulme, C. and Bradley, L. (1984). An experimental
study of multi-sensory teaching with normal and
retarded readers. In R. N. Malatesha and H. A.
Whitaker (eds.), Dyslexia: a global issue. The
Hague: Martinus Nijhoff.
Jansky, J. and de Hirsch, K. (1972). Preventing
reading failure - prediction, diagnosis,
intervention. New York: Harper and Row.
Jorm, A. F. (1977). Effect of word imagery on
reading performance as a function of reader
ability. Journal of Educational Psychology, 69,
51.
Jorm, A. F. (1979a). The cognitive and
neurological basis of developmental dyslexia: a
theoretical framework and review. Cognition, 7,
19 - 33.
Jorm, A. F. (1979b). The nature of the reading

deficit in developmental dyslexia: a reply to Ellis. Cognition, 9, 421 - 433.

Kennedy, H. (1942). A study of children's hearing as it relates to reading. Journal of Experimental Education, 10, 283 - 5.

Kinsbourne, M. (1970). The cerebral basis of lateral asymmetries in attention. Acta Psychologia, 33, 193 - 201.

Kinsbourne, M. and Warrington, E. K. (1966). Developmental factors in reading and writing backwardness. In J. Money (ed.), The disabled reader: education of the disabled child. Baltimore: Johns Hopkins University Press.

LaBerge, D. and Samuels, J. (1974). Toward a theory of automatic information processing in reading. Cognitive Psychology, 6, 293 - 323.

Labov, W. (1973). The logic of nonstandard English. In N. Keddie (ed.), Tinker, tailor .. The myth of cultural deprivation. Harmondsworth: Penguin.

Lachmann, F. M. (1960). Perceptual-motor development in children retarded in reading ability. Journal of Consulting Psychology, 24, 427 - 431.

Lambert, A. J. (1982). Right hemisphere language ability: 1. Clinical evidence. Current Psychological Reviews, 2, 77 - 94.

Laosa, L. M. (1982). School, occupation, culture and family: the impact of parental schooling on the parent-child relationship. Journal of Educational Psychology, 74, 791 - 827.

Lecours, A. R. (1975). Myelogenetic correlates of the development of speech and language. In E. H. Lenneberg (ed.), Foundations of language development: a multidisciplinary approach. (vol. 1). New York: Academic Press.

Love, H. D. (1970). Parents diagnose and correct reading problems: For parents of children with reading disabilities. Springfield, Ill: Thomas.

Lundberg, I., Olofsson, A. and Wall, S. (1980). Reading and spelling skills in kindergarten. Scandanavian Journal of Psychology, 21, 159 - 173.

Makita, K. (1968). The rarity of reading disability in Japanese children. American Journal of Orthopsychiatry, 38, 599 - 614.

Marcel, T. (1980). Surface dyslexia and beginning reading: a revised hypothesis of the pronunciation of print and its impairments. In M. Coltheart, K. Patterson and J. C. Marshall (eds.), Deep dyslexia. London: Routledge and

Kegan Paul.

Marin, O. S. M. (1980). Appendix 1. CAT scans of five deep dyslexic patients. In M. Coltheart, K. Patterson and J. C. Marshall (eds.), Deep dyslexia. London: Routledge and Kegan Paul.

Marshall, J. C. and Newcombe, F. (1973). Patterns of paralexia: a psycholinguistic approach. Journal of Psycholinguistic Research, 2, 175 - 199.

Martin, M., Schwyhart, K. and Wetzel, R. (1973). Teaching motivation in a high school reading program. In E. E. Ekwall (ed.), Psychological factors in the teaching of reading. Columbus, Ohio: Merrill.

Marwit, S., Marwit, K. and Boswell, J. (1972). Negro children's use of nonstandard grammar. Journal of Educational Psychology, 63, 218 - 24.

Mason, G. E. and Blanchard, J. S. (1979). Computer applications in reading. Newark, Del: International Reading Association.

Mattis, S., French, J. H. and Rapin, I. (1975). Dyslexia in children and young adults: three independent neuropsychological syndromes. Developmental Medicine and Child Neurology, 17, 150 - 163.

Meudell, P. (1981). Alexia, dyslexia and normal reading. In Pavlidis, G. Th. and Miles, T. R. (eds.), Dyslexia research and its applications to education. Chichester: John Wiley.

Miles, T. R. (ed.) (1978). Understanding dyslexia. London: Hodder and Stoughton.

Miller, G. W. (1970). Factors in school achievement and social class. Journal of Educational Psychology, 61, 260 - 69.

Morris, J. M. (1966). Standards and progress in reading. Slough: National Foundation for Educational Research.

Muehl, S. and Forell, E. R. (1973). A follow-up study of disabled readers: variables related to high school reading performance. Reading Research Quarterly, 9, 110 - 123.

Myklebust, H. R. and Johnson, D. J. (1962). Dyslexia in children. Exceptional Children, 29, 14 - 25.

Naylor, H. (1980). Reading disability and lateral asymmetry: an information processing analysis. Psychological Bulletin, 87, 531 - 545.

Neuman, S. B. (1981). Effect of teaching auditory perceptual skills on reading achievement in first grade. Reading Teacher, 34, 422 - 426.

Nicholson, R. (1981). The relationship between memory span and processing speed. In M. Friedman, J. P. Das and N. O'Connor (eds.), Intelligence and learning New York: Plenum.

Oakhill, J. (1982). Constructive processes in skilled and less skilled comprehenders' memory for sentences. British Journal of Psychology, 73, 13 - 20.

Oakhill, J. (1983). Instantiation in skilled and less skilled comprehenders. Quarterly Journal of Experimental Psychology, 35A, 441 - 450.

Patterson, K. E. (1979). What is right with deep dyslexic patients? Brain and Language, 8, 111 - 129.

Patterson, K. E. (1981). Neuropsychological approaches to the study of reading. British Journal of Psychology, 72, 151 - 174.

Patterson, K. E. and Kay, J. (1982). Letter-by-letter reading: psychological description of a neurological syndrome. Quarterly Journal of Psychology, 34A, 411 - 441.

Patterson, K. E. and Marcel, A. J. (1977). Aphasia, dyslexia and the phonological coding of written words. Quarterly Journal of Experimental Psychology, 29, 307 - 318.

Pavlidis, G. Th. (1981). Sequencing, eye movements and the early objective diagnosis of dyslexia. In G. Th. Pavlidis and T. R. Miles (eds.), Dyslexia research and its applications in education. Chichester: John Wiley.

Perfetti, C. A., Goldman, S. A. and Hogaboam, T. W. (1979). Reading skill and the identification of words in connected discourse. Memory and Cognition, 7, 273 - 282.

Perfetti, C. A. and Lesgold, A. (1978). Discourse comprehension and sources of individual differences. In M. Just and P. Carpenter (eds.), Cognitive processes in comprehension. Hillsdale, N. J.: Erlbaum.

Pirozzolo, F. J. and Hansch, E. C. (1982). The neurobiology of developmental reading disorders. In R. N. Malatesha and P. G. Aaron (eds.), Reading disorders: varieties and treatments. London: Academic Press.

Preston, M. S., Guthrie, J. T., Kirsch, I., Gertman, D. and Childs, B. (1977). VERs in normal and disabled adult readers. Psychophysiology, 14, 8 - 14.

Richardson, J. T. E. (1975a). The effect of word imageability in acquired dyslexia.

Neuropsychologia, 13, 281 - 288.

Richardson, J. T. E. (1975b). Further evidence on the effect of word imageability in dyslexia. Quarterly Journal of Psychology, 27, 445 - 449.

Richardson, J. T. E. (1976). The effects of stimulus attributes upon latency of word recognition. British Journal of Psychology, 67, 315 - 325.

Rosen, C. L. (1966). An experimental study of visual perceptual training and reading achievement in first grade. Perceptual and Motor Skills, 22, 979 - 986.

Rosen, C. L. (1968). An investigation of perceptual training and reading achievement in first grade. American Journal of Optometry, 45, 322 - 332.

Rubinstein, H., Lewis, S. S. and Rubinstein, M. A. (1971). Evidence for phonemic recoding in visual word recognition. Journal of Verbal Learning and Verbal Behavior, 10, 645 - 657.

Rutter, M. (1967). A children's behaviour questionnaire for completion by teachers: preliminary findings. Journal of Child Psychology and Psychiatry, 8, 1 - 11.

Rutter, M. (1978). Prevalence and types of dyslexia. In A. L. Benton and D. Pearl (eds.), Dyslexia: an appraisal of current knowledge. New York: Oxford University Press.

Rutter, M., Tizard, J. and Whitmore, K. (eds.), (1970). Education, Health and Behaviour. London: Longmans.

Saffran, E., Bogyo, L., Schwartz, M. and Marin, O. (1980). Does deep dyslexia reflect right hemisphere reading? In M. Coltheart, K. Patterson and J. Marshall (eds.), Deep dyslexia. London: Routledge and Kegan Paul.

Satz, P., Friel, J. and Rudegeair, F. (1974). Some predictive antecedents of specific reading disability: a two-, three-, and four-year follow up. In the Hyman Blumberg Symposium on Research in Early Childhood Education. Baltimore: Johns Hopkins University Press.

Satz, P. and Sparrow, S. (1970). Dyslexia, laterality and neuropsychological development. In D. J. Bakker and P. Satz (eds.), Specific reading disability: advances in theory and method. Rotterdam: Rotterdam University Press.

Satz, P., Taylor, G., Friel, J. and Fletcher, J. (1978). Some developmental and predictive precursors of reading disability: a six year follow up. In A. L. Benton and D. Pearl (eds.), Dyslexia: an appraisal of current knowledge. New York: Oxford University Press.

Seamon, J. G. and Gazzaniga, M. S. (1973). Coding strategies and cerebral laterality effects. Cognitive Psychology, 5, 249 - 256.

Shallice, T. and Warrington, E. K. (1975). Word recognition in a phonemic dyslexic patient. Quarterly Journal of Experimental Psychology, 27, 187 - 199.

Shearer, E. and Apps, R. (1975). A restandardization of the Burt-Vernon and Schonell Graded Word Reading Tests. Educational Research, 18, 67 - 73.

Shnayer, S. W. (1969). Relationships between reading interest and reading comprehension. In J. A. Figurel (ed.), Reading and realism. Newark, Del: International Reading Association.

Silver, A. (1978). Prevention. In A. L. Benton and D. Pearl (eds.), Dyslexia: an appraisal of current knowledge. New York: Oxford University Press.

Singer, M. H. and Crouse, J. (1981). The relationship of context-use skills to reading: a case for an alternative experimental logic. Child Development, 52, 1326 - 1329.

Smith, D. E. P. (1969). Increasing task behavior difficulty in a language - arts program by providing reinforcement. Journal of Experimental Child Psychology, 8, 45 - 62.

Snyder, R. D. and Warden, D. K. (1969). Failure of parental tutoring in childhood dyslexia. Clinical Pediatrics, 8, (8), 436.

Soderbergh, R. (1976). Learning to read between two and five: Some observations in normal hearing and deaf children. In C. Rameh (ed.), Semantics: theory and application. Washington, D.C.: Georgetown University Press.

Speddy, R. (1982). The Guinness pocket book of facts. Middlesex: Guinness Superlatives Ltd.

Stanley, G., Smith, G. A. and Howell, E. A. (1983). Eye-movements and sequential tracking in dyslexic and control children. British Journal of Psychology, 74, 181 - 187.

Start, K. B. and Wells, B. K. (1972). The trend of reading standards. Slough: National Foundation for Educational Research.

Sternberg, R. J. (1977). Writing the Psychology paper. Woodbury, NY: Barron's Educational Series.

Stevenson, N. (1974). The natural way to reading: a how-to method for parents of slow learners, dyslexics, and learning disabled children. Boston, Mass: Little, Brown.

Strag, G. (1972). Comparative behavioral ratings of parents with severe mentally retarded, special learning disability and normal children. Journal of Learning Disabilities, 5, 52 - 56.

Stroop, V. R. (1935). Studies of interference in serial reactions. Journal of Experimental Psychology, 18, 643 - 662.

Swadlow, H. A., Geschwind, N. and Waxman, S. G. (1979). Commissural transmission in humans. Science, 204, 530 - 31.

Symmes, J. S. and Rapoport, J. L. (1972). Unexpected reading failure. American Journal of Orthopsychiatry, 42, 82 - 91.

Thomson, M. E. and Grant, S. (1979). The WISC subtest profile of the dyslexic child. In M. Newton, M. Thomson and I. Richards (eds.), Readings in dyslexia. Wisbech, Cambs: LDA.

Tizard, J. (1972). Children with specific reading difficulties: report to the Advisory Committee on Handicapped Children. London: HMSO.

Tizard, J., Schofield, W. N. and Hewison, J. (1982). Collaboration between teachers and parents in assisting children's reading. British Journal of Educational Psychology, 52, 1 - 15.

Tuinman, J. J. (1973-74). Determining the passage dependency of comprehension questions in 5 major tests. Reading Research Quarterly, 9, 206 - 23.

Vellutino, F. R. (1977). Alternative conceptualizations of dyslexia: evidence in support of a verbal-deficit hypothesis. Harvard Educational Review, 47, 334 - 354.

Vellutino, F. R. (1979). Dyslexia: theory and research. Cambridge, Mass: MIT Press.

Vellutino, F. R., DeSetto, L. and Steger, J. A. (1972). Categorical judgement and the Wepman test of auditory discrimination. Journal of Speech and Hearing Disorders, 37, 252 - 7.

Vellutino, F. R., Smith, H., Steger, J. A. and Kaman, M. (1975). Reading disability: age differences and the perceptual-deficit hypothesis. Child Development, 46, 487 - 493.

Vinsonhaler, J. F., Weinshank, A. B., Wagner, C. C. and Polin, R. M. (1983). Diagnosing children with educational problems: characteristics of reading and learning disabilities specialists, and classroom teachers.

Reading Research Quarterly, 18, 134 - 164.

Wallach, M. A. and Wallach, L. (1976). Teaching all children to read. Chicago: University of Chicago Press.

Warburton, F. W. and Southgate, V. (1969). ita: an independent evaluation. London: Newgate Press Limited.

Warrington, E. K. (1967). The incidence of verbal disability associated with retardation in reading. Neuropsychologia, 5, 175 - 179.

Warrington, E. (1981). Concrete word dyslexia. British Journal of Psychology, 72, 175 - 198.

Warrington, E. K., Logue, V. and Pratt, R. T. C. (1971). The anatomical localization of selective impairment of auditory verbal short-term memory. Neuropsychologia, 9, 377 - 387.

Wechsler, D. (1949). Wechsler intelligence scale for children. New York: Psychological Corporation.

Wepman, J. M. (1958). The auditory discrimination test. Chicago: Language Research Associates.

Whittaker, E. M. (1982). Dyslexia and the flat earth. Bulletin of the British Psychological Society, 35, 97 - 98.

Wilkinson, A. C. (1983). Classroom computers and cognitive science. London: Academic Press.

Williams, P. A., Haertel, E. H., Haertel, G. D. and Walberg, H. J. (1982). The impact of leisure-time television on school learning: A research synthesis. American Educational Research Journal, 19, 19 - 50.

Wolf, M. (1982). An approach to the combined study of acquired and developmental reading disorders. In R. N. Malatesha and P. G. Aaron (eds.), Reading disorders: varieties and treatments. London: Academic Press.

Young, A. W. and Ellis, A. W. (1981). Asymmetry of cerebral hemispheric function in normal and poor readers. Psychological Bulletin, 89, 183 - 190.

Zifcak, M. (1981). Phonological awareness and reading acquisition. Contemporary Educational Psychology, 6, 117 - 126.

139

144

An up-to-date standardization
of the Schonell Reading Test

The Schonell Reading Test is no longer
entirely accurate in assessing the reading age of
children. It is probably not the best test of
reading to use either. For instance the Neale
Analysis of Reading takes into account standards
in comprehension by applying a comprehension test
after the child reads a passage as well as
assessing basic reading skill. However the
Schonell is still widely used. I have conducted a
computer search (in 1983) of the Psychological
Abstracts and found that the most recent
standardization of the Schonell has been by
Shearer and Apps (1975). test
after the child reads a passage as well as
assessing basic reading skill. However the
Schonell is still widely used. I have conducted a
computer search (in 1983) of the Psychological
Abstracts and found that the most recent
standardization of the Schonell has been by
Shearer and Apps (1975). Their conversion table
is reproduced in Table Al below. I hope that
teachers and professionals alike will find this
useful for making more accurate assessments of
reading age. To use the table, if the child is
only able to read nine words correctly on the
test, the reading age according to Table Al is 5
years and 11 months. The restandardization was
based on a stratified sample of 2000 children in
Cheshire, England. A previous survey in 1971
revealed that a sample of children from Cheshire
second-year junior children were of the same
reading standard as obtained nationally using the
NFER Sentence Reading Test 2.

Table A1
A restandardization of the Schonell
graded word reading test

Reading age	Conversion to reading ages based on a survey of Cheshire children											
	Months											
Years	0	1	2	3	4	5	6	7	8	9	10	11
5	–	–	1	2	3	4	4	5	6	7	8	9
6	10	11	11	12	13	14	15	16	17	18	18	19
7	20	21	22	23	24	25	25	26	27	28	29	30
8	31	32	32	33	34	35	36	37	38	39	39	40
9	41	42	43	44	45	46	46	47	48	49	50	51
10	52	53	53	54	55	56	57	58	59	60	60	61
11	62											